ON BEING
GAY

ON BEING

GAY

THOUGHTS ON FAMILY, FAITH, AND LOVE

BRIAN McNAUGHT

ST. MARTIN'S PRESS
NEW YORK

Design by Judith Stagnitto.

Library of Congress Cataloging-in-Publication Data

McNaught, Brian.
On being gay / by Brian McNaught.
p. cm.
ISBN 0-312-01800-2
1. Gays—Psychology.   I. Title.
HQ76.25.M375 1988   87-36687
306.7′662—dc19   CIP

First Edition

10 9 8 7 6 5 4 3 2 1

CONTENTS

FOREWORD   ix
INTRODUCTION   xi

ON BEING YOURSELF   1

Dear Anita: Late Night Thoughts of an Irish Catholic
    Homosexual   5
Coming Out—The Price   15
Coming Out—The Payoff   18
Oppressing Ourselves   21
More Pluses   25
The Next Step   28
Living for Yourself   31
A Celebration of Self   36

GROWING UP GAY   41

High School Horrors   44
The Prom   48
Courage on Campus   51
Class Reunion   55
The March   58

My Family   61
A Trip to the Gym   64
Reclaiming the Holidays   68
Proud Growls and Courageous Roars   72
I Like It   76

FRIENDS AND LOVERS   79

Defining Community   82
Understanding Sexism   85
Making Allies of Married Gays   89
Sick of Hearing About AIDS   93
Meeting New People   97
How to Find a Lover   101
Making It Last   105
Monogamy   113
Open Relationships   116
Life's Real Meaning   119
The Letter in the Desk   123
Despite It All, We Love   127

THE JOURNEY FORWARD   131

The Sad Dilemma of the Gay Catholic   134
But Do You Love the Church?   146
Duplicity   150
Forgiveness   155
Listening to the Voice Within   159
Serenity versus Security   163

CELEBRATION 167

Proud About What? 171

FOREWORD

This is a very special book by someone we consider to be a very special man. It is our experience that when gay people read Brian McNaught's words or hear him speak, they end up feeling better about themselves. When heterosexuals have the same experience, they at the very least come away with a far richer understanding of what it means to be gay—if, in fact, they don't end up feeling better about being human.

What sets this book apart from most other books about homosexuality we've seen is not the facts, although all of the important facts are here. As a highly acclaimed sex educator, Brian has a comprehensive knowledge of his subject. However, facts are facts and other books have them, too. What he adds to the facts are the feelings of being gay. In this regard, he has set himself apart. From this book and from his other efforts, we get from Brian McNaught an intimate look at what it was like wrestling with same-sex thoughts as a child. We remember, if we are gay, or learn if we are not, what it was like attempting to reconcile our religious thoughts with our sexual feelings. We come out again; we go into our first gay bar; we fall in love; we deal with our families; we struggle with the Church; we confront AIDS. We grow from the frightened child into the self-affirmed adult. Being gay is far more than being physically attracted to persons of the same gender. It is a way of being in the world, and Brian McNaught captures that for us.

Within this book, and within his life, you will find encouragement to be who you are and permission to be proud. We think you will find reading this book to be a special experience.

Andrew Mattison, Ph.D.
David McWhirter, M.D.
Coauthors,
The Male Couple

INTRODUCTION

When *A Disturbed Peace*,—the title of my earlier book in which many of these essays first appeared—was published in 1981, the questions I heard most about homosexuality were pretty basic—"How do I know if I'm gay? Can I change it? Who should I tell? Will I be happy?" To my great pleasure, the collection of my writings seemed to comfort and encourage those who were able to find my book, and to answer in a non-threatening and supportive way their inquiries about what it means to be gay.

Back then, my life and that of most adult gay men and lesbian women in this country was very different than it is to-day. The biggest difference, of course, is that none of us were aware of AIDS. Our attitudes about much of our lives have been greatly altered by that deadly virus, if for no other reason than we have faced our own mortality every time we buried another friend in his twenties or thirties. Other factors had their effects too, such as the Supreme Court's five to four decision to uphold a state's right to prosecute private, consensual gay sexuality; the Vatican's decree on homosexuality; and the effects of President Ronald Reagan's conservative domestic agenda. The success of *A Disturbed Peace*, which seems to have deeply touched the lives of many people, merited republishing in a somewhat revised form for a broader audience. The events in the culture warranted an expansion of the original text. The result is *On Being Gay*.

The many changes which I see in myself and in the gay and lesbian community since I sat down ten years ago to write an open letter to antigay crusader Anita Bryant are very positive and exciting. Despite all of the negative influences which I could cite, or perhaps because of them, a multitude of gay men and lesbian women have emerged as self-affirmed, self-determined and self-reliant individuals. Society, too, has grown to better understand and appreciate the great diversity and strength of gay people. Since this book first appeared, for instance, *La Cage aux Folles*, *Torch Song Trilogy*, *Kiss of the Spider Woman*, *The Life and Times of Harvey Milk* and other gay-theme works have been recognized with public honors. Once considered an "invisible minority," gay people are more likely to be portrayed honestly in the media and in the arts today than we were a decade ago, although the picture is still far from complete.

The AIDS crisis is partly responsible for this new visibility, for two reasons. AIDS was the catalyst for the creation of one of the largest volunteer efforts this country has ever seen. Gay men and lesbian women from Maine to Hawaii stepped forward to help meet the financial and physical needs of the thousands of persons with AIDS and AIDS-Related Complex (ARC), and to educate the rest of society about reducing the risk of infection. This brought a new sophistication and sense of purpose to a group of people who had hungered for a keener sense of community. The media recorded some of this emergence, resulting in the presentation of new positive role models. Also, faced with the deaths of so many young gay friends, gay men and women have been forced to make some decisions. We have had to clarify for ourselves the essence of being gay, to individually determine its importance in our lives with respect to our need for acceptance and security and to examine carefully how we planned not only to survive but to grow. That decision making resulted in far more people coming out of the closet and affirming publicly their pride in being gay. (Hundreds of thousands did so in a massive march on Washington, D.C., in October of 1987.) What needed to be added, then, to a revised edition of the earlier book were new thoughts on survival and new ideas about the direction in which we are heading.

Some things in the book, however, needed to stay the same. The facts about homosexuality offered in *A Disturbed Peace* are intact. Those facts are so important in helping all of us get rid of our myths, our misunderstandings and our fears. Also remaining are the personal stories from my past which apparently record for a good many people the feelings of their growing-up years, too. Much has changed in the world for adult gay men and lesbian women, but the experience of growing up gay, with some variations, remains the same. Although an entire generation of gay men and women have emerged who have no knowledge of Anita Bryant, they do know the sense of isolation and fear, alienation and hurt which every generation of gay men and women has felt. Though it would seem they are blooming in a world with far more opportunities for gay people than ever before, they are still confronted with the familiar agonizing questions: "How do I know if I'm gay? Is it a stage? Should I tell anyone? Will my parents still love me? Can I change? What did I do to cause this? Does God not love me? Will I be happy? Is it possible to have a relationship? What about my career? If I marry, will these feelings go away? Will I fit in as a gay person? Is there anything special I have to do to be truly gay?" And now, "Will I die if I kiss someone?"

Likewise, despite all of the advances we have made as a society in better understanding the full spectrum of human sexuality, the parents of these young people are tossing and turning at night with the same questions asked by my parents: "Why is this happening? What did I do wrong? Who have you told? How can I change this? Will you be happy?" It is primarily with these young people in mind, their parents, family and friends, those who teach them and who minister to their needs, that we have worked for the revision and expansion of *A Disturbed Peace* into this volume, *On Being Gay*.

On Being Gay is a collection of articles selected from those I have written for thirteen years in the gay and mainstream press. "Dear Anita," for instance, first appeared in a national sex-education journal *(Impact)*. "The Sad Dilemma of the Gay Catholic," was written for a national Catholic magazine, the *U.S. Catholic*. "Forgiveness" was written for *The Witness*, an Episcopal Church periodical. The remaining articles were columns I wrote in syndication for the gay press. Eighteen new columns have been added to this collection, while a few original ones have been deleted. The articles have been dated so that the reader can trace the development of identity and also see how some basic beliefs remained constant. These included the thought that "the essence of being gay is being who you truly are."

The response to *A Disturbed Peace* was highly gratifying. Originally published by Dignity, Inc., an organization of gay Catholics, the book went into three printings and sold, through very limited distribution, several thousand copies. I am really pleased with its success in comforting and encouraging people who needed a little help cutting through the fear. Now I'm delighted to know that *On Being Gay* has the opportunity to support an even broader audience in its quest for understanding, acceptance and affirmation.

This book is dedicated to Ray Struble, my intimate partner in life since 1976. Despite all of the other changes, that joyfully remains the same.

O N B E I N G
YOURSELF

ON BEING
YOURSELF

Before we can begin to love ourselves, which I believe is crucial for sound mental health and total union with God, we have to root out the negative stereotypes with which we were raised, and begin to build positive self-images. Once we have identified ourselves as gay or lesbian and affirmed it as an essential ingredient to our uniqueness, we face the question: "Who else do we tell?" Coming out of the closet is one of the most important steps a gay person can take and it is a lifelong process. It has a big price tag, but for the overwhelming majority of people, it has an even bigger payoff. However, it shouldn't be done without a support system. Having come out, we emerge into the gay and lesbian community, where we are frequently greeted with a barrage of opinions of what it means to be "truly gay." What we call ourselves, how we dress and talk and the components of our love relationships are considered important, but the real essence of being gay is being who you truly are. There is no secret formula or mode of behavior which makes one person more gay than another. Once a person has learned to be himself or herself, being gay becomes a gift and life becomes an opportunity to explore and celebrate.

Editor's Note: In the summer of 1977, singer and Florida orange juice spokeswoman Anita Bryant spearheaded a successful campaign to rescind gay rights legislation in Dade County, Florida. It was a bitter battle which mobilized Christian fundamentalists and Orthodox Jews on one side and the nation's gay and lesbian community on the other. To her supporters, Anita Bryant was a modern-day Joan of Arc battling for the integrity of the American family. To the supporters of gay and lesbian civil rights, she was a dangerous, misguided woman whose name became synonymous with antigay bigotry. Following the Dade County vote, there was a spate of progay civil rights ordinances which were either overturned or rejected.

DEAR ANITA

Late Night Thoughts of an Irish Catholic Homosexual

October 1978

I am a thirty-year-old Irish Catholic middle child of a family of seven. My father recently retired from the General Motors public relations staff. My mother now enjoys the peace of an empty house. My older brothers and sisters are married with children; my younger brothers and sisters are "searching for the meaning of life."

I had sixteen years of parochial education. The nuns considered me a "prince of a boy." I was patrol boy of the year, played high school basketball, was senior class president and editor of the Marquette University yearbook. Recently I was named one of the "Outstanding Young Men in America" and was asked by a national magazine to share with others the development of what is considered an intense spirituality.

You and I share the same values, Anita. I, too, am afraid to walk the streets at night. I abhor pornography and drugs. I detest the rat race, the unemployment, the breakdown of the family, the incidence of illegitimate births and the inability of many school children to read and write. I, too, take the phone off the hook during the "Waltons." I, too, miss "Star Trek." I, too, cried during the final segment of "Mary Tyler Moore." If you didn't know I was a homosexual, you would insist that I be at all your parties because "Brian has a great sense of humor." We would be praying together and playing together and you would pay extra to make sure it was I who babysat your children.

Let me assure you that I know you truly believe that your crusade is God's crusade. I also totally understand your fear, disgust or apprehension about homosexuality. Both of us have been raised since we were little to believe that: (1) God condemns homosexuality; (2) homosexuality is a psychiatric disorder; (3) male homosexuals hate women and are sexually interested in children. We also learned that male homosexuals wish they were women and lesbians wish they were men.

If all that frightens you, think for a minute what it did to me as I grew up with the secret knowledge that for some unknown reason I was physically attracted to men.

I read the same Bible you read. I heard the same sick jokes you heard. For that reason, I never identified myself as homosexual. I couldn't be, I thought. I have shelves loaded with swimming trophies. I dated throughout high school and college and seriously considered getting married on three occasions. Homosexuals were supposed to be interested in children and I find the very thought abhorrent, and the closest thing to women's apparel I have ever worn was the outfit every altar boy wore.

Was I psychologically unbalanced? Well, for several years I thought about entering the seminary or monastery. Every time you apply to a Roman Catholic religious order, they screen you by having you examined by a psychiatrist. With each interview I would reveal my homosexual feelings and without exception every psychiatrist told me it wasn't a problem. My only problem, they told me, was living in a hostile world.

Eventually I did enter the monastery but the scenario was similar to the one played out in *The Sound of Music* . . . you know, "always late for chapel but his penitence is real. Always late for everything except for every meal." After a while we concluded together that "Brian's not an asset to the Abbey."

Back at Marquette I was a daily Mass-goer. I read the lessons and led the congregation in song. I was labeled "dormitory Catholic" and "the saint." It didn't bother me. Faith is a way of life. Spirituality is an action verb.

Do you know that I didn't have any sexual encounters until I was twenty-one? Most of the men in my class lost their virginity in high school, some earlier. But the "saint" didn't. It wasn't until he "experimented" with another lonely, frightened male student who was also a virgin that he knew what all the excitement was about. It was awkward and mechanical for both of us and ended with expressions of gratitude because it was so uncomfortable we both knew we couldn't possibly be *real* homosexuals.

Jim and I both, however, unbeknownst to each other, continued to have male-oriented fantasies. He asked if we might try it again and, being the rational creature that I am, I insisted that I had to have a heterosexual experience before I ever had another one which was homosexual, so that I would know whether or not I had unknowingly closed myself off.

The following year, I did have my first heterosexual experience with a wonderfully patient and sensitive woman. Despite my earnest desire to enjoy it, thereby removing myself from a life of secrets, shadows and stereotypes, I could not experience physical pleasure.

Now doctors and the theologians of my Church say I am what is called a "constitutional" homosexual as distinguished from a "transitional" homosexual. This means that my sexual orientation was set before I was old enough to know what was going on. They say age three to five. The only memory I have of being five is making bean-bag puppets in Tot Lot and vague recollections of splashing around in Allen Goldstein's plastic swimming pool. But, they say, that's when it all occurred. They have conducted all sorts of surveys and tests to determine what causes a person's sexual orientation, not unlike the studies they used to make to figure out why some people are left-handed when the majority of the population is right-handed.

Do you know what they found, Anita? Nothing. Every study contradicted the other. All they know is that 10 percent of the population is exclusively or predominantly homosexual in orientation. That's twenty-two million Americans.

I mentioned *transitional homosexual*. This term describes an individual who is basically heterosexual but who also engages in homosexual behavior when there are no persons of the opposite gender available, such as in prison or the armed forces. Once

they are out of those circumstances, they revert back to heterosexual behavior.

Human sexuality, in my view, is a beautiful gift, which
like all gifts can be and has been abused. It's like your gift of
voice. You can use that gift to create beautiful, inspiring songs
which uplift people's spirits or you can sing songs which upset
people. You can sing upon request or you can force people to
hear your singing when they don't feel up to it. You alone determine when and how you are going to use it.

There was a time when it was taught that the sole purpose
of human sexuality was procreation of the species. Women were
instructed to lie perfectly still and even refrain from enjoying
what was happening. The slightest enjoyment was considered
sinful.

Today, we say that human sexuality can be procreative but
that it doesn't have to be. We rejoice at the wedding of a young
or elderly couple who for one reason or another are incapable of
having children. We wouldn't think of asking them to refrain
from expressing their love to each other without the gift of sexuality. We know by our studies of infants that every human
person needs to be held and stroked. We know that without
human warmth, an infant can die or become seriously malad-
justed.

We also know that sexual expression is a language. It can
mean a variety of things, from I love you, I need you, I'm
lonely, I'm hurt, to I hate you. The most beautiful expression
of human sexuality is when it communicates selfless love. The
most abhorrent is rape. Between the two, there is a whole spectrum of meanings and values.

Secondly, I would dare to say that I have studied and
prayed through Scripture with the same excitement and interest
as you have. Your God is my God. Your spiritual goal is my
spiritual goal. Your hope is my hope. But we both know how
easy it is to abuse Scripture. Slave owners used it to justify
slavery. Catholics used it to torture and kill Protestants. Christians continue to use it to condemn Jews. We are weak human
beings who frequently look to the Bible for justification of our
position, our fears and even our hatred.

Who today pays any attention to Leviticus: 11 when they
sit down to a lobster dinner or New England clam chowder?

Who stones the woman caught in adultery as the Bible insists? Who believes that people get married because they can't control their lust? What priest or minister has ever been denied ordination because he or she had a hernia operation, a crooked nose or humped back? Do we burn red dresses? Do we hang St. Paul's haircutting specifications in our barbershops and beauty salons? Rather, don't we explain that much of the Bible has to be understood in a cultural context? Anita, you know that the Old Testament Jews prepared their meals the day before the Sabbath because work was absolutely forbidden on the Sabbath. When was the last time any of us fried eggs and bacon on a Saturday night for Sunday brunch?

Why then do we quote Genesis, Leviticus and St. Paul's letters to Romans, Corinthians and Timothy as justification of our belief that God abhors homosexuality? Scripture scholars insist that every one of those passages has been taken out of context. No one understood the concept of *constitutional homosexuality* until sixty years ago. The Jewish writers of the Old Testament and St. Paul in the New had no idea that anyone by nature was homosexual in orientation. They presumed that everyone was heterosexual and that those engaging in homosexual behavior were heterosexuals mimicking pagan rites, which was tantamount to idolatry. These findings are not by closeted homosexuals who seek justification of their lifestyle. The scholars in question have pursued the accurate interpretation in every area of Scripture. What good is the message of God if it is misunderstood?

In your book and in your national campaign you state your opposition to homosexuals teaching in schools. You and I both know that homosexuals have been teaching in classrooms for centuries. You have told the American people that homosexuals want to wear dresses to school. Wearing the clothing of the opposite gender is called transvestism, and while there are some gay men who have and do on occasion wear women's attire, the majority of transvestites are heterosexual males. And yet, given these statistics, no one is suggesting that heterosexual male teachers wish to wear their wives' clothing to math class.

Likewise with your comments about child molestation. Persons who are sexually interested in children are called pederasts and I am sure you have heard of the studies which show that the overwhelming majority of pederasts are heterosexuals. Usually the case involves a father with his young daughter. Do we take this information from police blotters and then suggest that all heterosexuals are child molesters? No. That would be absurd. But that's what you are telling the country about homosexuals, and many people seem to believe you.

When you say, Anita, that gay civil rights will prompt homosexuals to flaunt their lifestyles, what do you mean? Do you mean that a homosexual teacher, assigned to teach history, will spend class time describing his or her relationship at home? If that is what you are opposed to, I join you in your crusade. A teacher is hired to instruct students in a specific area of learning. But is that what you mean by "flaunting"?

Isn't the whole battle really centered upon your opposition to the gay man or woman affirming himself or herself as being a happy, healthy, normal, country-loving, God-fearing human sexual being? This is what gay people are saying the whole battle is for them. We are simply saying that we are unable to live healthy, productive lives in a society which insists we are sick and sinful people.

Let me make the case more understandable by bringing it closer to home. Let's for the sake of argument say that your thirteen-year-old son Bob, Jr., has strong homosexual feelings. What does it mean? It means that even if you asked him about it, he couldn't or wouldn't talk with you. This would probably upset you, especially if you knew there was something troubling him that he didn't feel secure enough to share with his mother. I have watched you closely, Anita, given all the press coverage, and am impressed with your devotion to your family. Playing and praying together are essential ingredients in creating a family unit which will be something a child can look to for support throughout his or her life. My folks did the same and have reaped a family strength which is the envy of many of their friends.

But even given that security, Bob, Jr., couldn't and wouldn't talk with you about his homosexual feelings. He couldn't because he wouldn't understand them himself. He would be aware of the fact that while watching television or looking through books or swimming at the country club he was inexplicably excited by the sight of a handsome man, but he couldn't put a label on it. Even if he could, he wouldn't talk with you about it because your love and Bob's love mean everything in the world to him and he would never say anything which might threaten that.

Therein lies the tragedy of being a homosexual in today's society. What makes it even worse is that despite his homosexual feelings, chances are that Bob, Jr., really isn't a constitutional homosexual. Kinsey revealed in his studies that while close to 10 percent of the total population is predominantly or exclusively homosexual, 37 percent of the American male population have homosexual experiences and 50 percent, homosexual fantasies. This means that well over 20 percent of those having homosexual experiences are not actually homosexual by nature. But because we don't talk about it, because the subject is taboo, they don't know that.

Getting back to Bob, Jr., though, let's presume that he is homosexual. (You may say this is an absurd argument because you are sure he isn't. My parents would have said the same thing because I defied every stereotype.) Who is your son supposed to talk to? He doesn't understand what's happening to him. At that age, he would probably change if he could, but he can't. Does he approach your minister? We know what kind of reception he would get and so does he. Is there a gay teacher at school whom he respects? Probably not. There are undoubtedly gay teachers at his school but they won't admit it for fear of being fired.

Bob, Jr., is alone in the world. For year after year he carries this heavy psychological burden. He likes himself and hates himself. He decides to date and probably really enjoys the company of his girl friends, but he just isn't interested in heavy kissing and is incredibly uncomfortable in any situation where that is expected of him. He jokes in the locker room and laughs with his friends about his mother's comments on Adam and Bruce in the Garden of Eden. He calls his classmates who are weak and effeminate "queer." He even roughs one up to prove his masculinity.

Family and friends praise him for his looks and kid him about his being a real "lady-killer." He watches the smiles of pride that you and Bob have on your faces. What a fine man Bob, Jr., is turning out to be. Inside, he is tearing his guts to shreds. "If they only knew. If they only knew."

The scenario is similar in college. His moodiness bothers

you a bit at times but you presume that it is the pressures of school and career choices. What actually bothers him is the pedestal he's been put on and the expectation that everyone has of him to eventually settle down with the Breck girl and produce 2.75 healthy children.

If he makes it this far, then he has some major decisions to come to grips with. I say if he makes it this far because the chances are good that he will kill himself before he has to choose to hurt you. Suicide is the number one cause of death of young gay people. A bullet to the head ("He was cleaning his gun"); crashing the car into a concrete overpass ("He must have lost control"); an overdose of drugs ("He wasn't that kind of boy. Someone must have forced him"); or he can die emotionally by abandoning his dreams and accepting the sick and sinful label as a lifelong curse.

I was lucky, Anita. After I drank the bottle of paint thinner and consumed the bottle of pills, I changed my mind. I drove to the hospital and had my stomach pumped. As the tears rolled down the cheeks of "the saint," I vowed never again to live my life based upon the expectations of others. Given a choice, I felt they would prefer me to be a living homosexual than a dead question mark. Some people in this country, as we both know, would prefer I hadn't changed my mind.

But not you, Anita. Beneath all of that rhetoric is a basic belief in God. It was our God that I wanted to go home to when I drank the paint thinner. I felt like a kid at camp who couldn't cope with the hostility of the counselors and the other campers. Every day was a nightmare. If God wasn't going to come to camp and pick me up, I was going to run away and explain it all later. I changed my mind when I decided that I had paid the same price to attend camp as every other kid and that camp rules prohibited the counselors from acting like God.

If the Bob, Jr., of our story never chose to commit suicide, he would have to choose whether or not to marry. If he marries, he will fantasize about men while having sex with his wife. (Many of the people I counsel are married men with several children. They have been able to perform sexually by pretending that it was another man they were relating to.) If he chooses not to marry a woman, then he can attempt to be celibate (a goal which has met with little success) or he can seek out a companion with whom he wishes to share his life.

Anita, let's say that Bob, Jr., comes home and finally and tearfully tells you that he is a homosexual. I heard you say on CBS's "Who's Who" that if that happened you would tell your son that you love him. I know that you would. You would tell him that you love him as much now as you did before. He continues to cry and tells you and Bob how hard it has been for him and how he didn't want to hurt you and how he feels so relieved that you both now know. He has missed being part of the family and asks if it is okay to tell the other three children.

Into the house walks a family friend, who, in the midst of a conversation begins talking about "queers" making gains in New York City. Bob, Jr., is sitting quietly with you, attempting to refrain from showing any reaction. The conversation continues. "Those faggots want to dress in women's clothing, molest our children, flaunt their homosexuality," and so on.

Do you sit and listen quietly? Do you interrupt and change the subject? What is your husband's reaction? When you have your answer, Anita, you will know exactly how my parents and forty-four million other parents in this country react when they hear you on television or read your comments about their children in the newspaper.

What is Bob, Jr.'s reaction? Does he begin to water at the eyes? Does he storm out of the house with thoughts of suicide, revenge, hate, disappointment with you, or pride? You know your son. What is his reaction? When you have that answer, Anita, you will know how I felt inside and how twenty-two million other Americans felt when they watched the results of Dade County, St. Paul, Wichita and Eugene and when they listen to you speak.

I knew that we were going to lose in Dade County et al., because people don't understand what "gay pride" is all about. They mistakenly see it as one more threat to stable American life. But if you and your family experienced the real psychological terror that Bob, Jr., would go through as a homosexual, you would understand what this "gay civil rights movement" is all about.

It is a primal scream, Anita, by millions of people who want to live. It is an angry denunciation of all of the lies which have been heaped upon us for as long as we can remember. It is a pleading to straight society to refrain from forcing us to live in shadows of self-hate. What could be more inhumane?

Gay civil rights are human civil rights. Competent people should not be denied jobs because of what they do as consenting adults in the privacy of their homes. People should not be denied shelter because of inherent feelings they have had since they were children.

If you want to go on a national campaign against any person who molests children, against any person who recruits children, against any person who sexually forces himself or herself upon another, against any person who is not doing what he or she was hired to do, you will have my talents, energy and money behind you. Homosexuals, however, have nothing to fear from such a crusade.

What homosexuals and every other person under the sun fear is being stereotyped. One band instructor who sodomizes boys is no more an indictment of homosexuality than Hitler's hate for the Jews is for all of Germany; the Ku Klux Klan's hatred of blacks is for all Southerners; the Boston Strangler is for all heterosexuals; Sirhan Sirhan is for all Arabs or Joseph McCarthy is for all Catholics. Nor should a gay person affirming himself or herself be construed as "flaunting" any more than black persons affirming their blackness; Christians affirming their faith or a woman affirming her uniqueness as a woman.

We are all unique, Anita. Each of us is called to develop our unique talents, totally reflecting the wholeness of our being. No one has the right to deny that process unless it truly interferes with the rights of others.

You state that gay civil rights infringes upon your right as a mother to raise your child in a healthy society. But the healthiest society is that which protects people from blind fear of others and guarantees them the right to life, liberty and the pursuit of happiness. To challenge that is to challenge not only the cornerstone of this country, which we both claim to love, but also the very fiber of our faith, which we both claim to follow.

I will join you in prayer tonight, Anita, requesting that those who suffer might be comforted and that those who are comfortable might be disturbed by the suffering of others.

COMING OUT—
THE PRICE

August 1979

Five years ago, when I came out publicly, I was fired by a woman who was my editor and second mother at a Catholic newspaper. One day last week I received in the mail from her a box containing the "stuff" which I had left behind in my desk.

My first impulse was to throw the box away without looking at its contents. Losing my job and all of the security surrounding it was the most painful experience of my life and I wasn't sure I wanted to take the chance of ripping open that wound. Yet, I was curious and feeling brave (Ray was nearby paging through our photo album), so I began shuffling through the random assortment of memorabilia.

At different times, most especially in the beginning, the process was an exciting journey through a time tunnel. My 1974 capsule contained two eight-cent stamps; a trophy I won from the Heart Fund for riding forty miles in the Cyclethon; a letter from the Selective Service releasing me from any further obligation as a conscientious objector; a copy of my letter to Peter Rodino, chairperson of the House Judiciary Committee, in which I requested Richard Nixon's impeachment; a pile of addressed but unstamped Christmas cards; my Social Security card and Wilma Koslowski's recipe for coffee cake.

There were also copies of columns and articles I had written and several notebooks of half-sentences from my various reporting assignments. (In one such notebook my writing abruptly ends with a long, undirected line of ink which falls off the page. That must be from the time I fell asleep while interviewing the bishop. Thank goodness he didn't notice.)

As I had feared, my journey through the box was also very painful. It started me thinking about the good times I had had at the paper; about the laughs with the friends I had made in my four years there; about my career and my great hopes for the future. I thought about how proud my folks were and how excited my nieces and nephews got when they saw their names in my column. I thought about Margaret, the woman who fired me, and how I felt I was a surrogate son to replace the one my age she had lost. I thought about Mildred, the black woman who used to strike up an old song for me to join in every time I walked through her typesetting room. I began to wonder again, as I have so frequently in the last five years, why it all had to end the way it did.

A couple of days later I met Paul Guilbert. Paul is the young Rhode Island high school junior who made international headlines when it was learned he planned to take his boyfriend to the school prom.

Before introducing myself, I imagined what kinds of things must now be happening to Paul. Since his name became a household word, I imagined Paul was now receiving lots of letters from all over the world. I imagined he was being asked to speak at rallies, classroom discussions and gay conferences. I imagined he was suddenly surrounded by people who would be happy to sleep with him, to discuss the movement with him or, at the very least, to call him friend. I wondered how his teenage life had changed and I thought about the box he might be shuffling through in five years—a box containing little reminders of where he had been in 1979, a place to which he could never return.

After hearing from him that he was well and happy, though he would be changing schools for his senior year, I offered Paul a big piece of unsolicited advice. "Paul," I said, "what you did was very important and will undoubtedly make it that much easier for others to follow. I am sure you are being inundated with praise and attention and you should enjoy every minute of it while it lasts. You deserve it. But be careful. You owe it to yourself to get your education, to enjoy the rest of high school and college, to build a personal and professional life of your own. Don't get swallowed up in the movement. The best contribution you can make is to develop yourself to your full potential and to be happy. Do you know what I'm talking about?"

Paul smiled his seventeen-year-old smile. Before he had much of a chance to respond, his attention was being sought by another.

Paul Guilbert is a hero today to a lot of people who want to come out but are afraid. While most of these people, like Paul, would prefer not to make headlines, they would like to have the courage to ask a person of the same sex to the high school prom or the fraternity barn boozer or the holiday staff party. And there are still a lot of people who would be happy just to come out privately to family and friends.

The process of coming out is probably never-ending. I thought it was finished when I made it into *The New York Times*, but five years later I still have to make daily decisions about coming out while buying flowers, leaving for airplanes and walking in the park. The process begins with self-affirmation, that important first step when we acknowledge our same-sex feelings. When that acknowledgment becomes self-acceptance, we begin to share the information with those people in our lives who either need to know or who we want to know.

Coming out to family and friends has been shown to be a positive political gesture. In studies conducted among persons voting on gay civil rights, individuals who knew a gay person were shown generally to be far more supportive than those who didn't. Likewise, coming out can be a positive step toward sound mental health. However, as much as I would like to see every gay person and bisexual person declare publicly his or her orientation, I think it important we caution the overly anxious about the possible personal ramifications at this time in history.

The more you come out, the greater your freedom. The greater your freedom, the greater the price you pay. After all, "freedom's just another word for nothin' left to lose."

COMING OUT—
THE PAYOFF

August 1980

Michael, your Mom doesn't believe you're dead. She wants you to know you can go home. If you're gay, it's okay with her. She loves you.

Being gay is no reason for dying. Spread the word: Being gay is a good reason for living. The time has come to totally eliminate death as a dangling modifier of "gay." Why are they so related?

Recent studies have shown that the majority of gay people who die violent deaths are closeted. Further, a considerable number of killers of homosexuals are other closeted homosexuals. Another group of gay people, many of whom are young, commit suicide. Michael totally disappeared. His friends think he's dead. His mother thinks he vanished in order to be gay. That's dying too.

I tried to commit suicide once because I couldn't deal with being gay. I also considered disappearing so that I could escape a life of expectations. I've never put myself in a position of being killed by a closeted homosexual, but I understand why some people do. Sex with a stranger, they reason, means no one can trace you.

Last night I had dinner with a young guy who inherited $150,000 from a grandparent, but his father, who is executor of the will, refuses to give him the money until he stops all of this "gay foolishness." He walked away from that inheritance and from a $40,000-a-year job in order to begin being a whole person at age twenty-six. Does he have any regrets? He's as poor as a church mouse now and would love to have a steady income, but he would never trade his discovery of wholeness for the price tag on the closet door.

The connection between gay deaths and the blossoming gay young man is that many homosexuals die because they fear they can't handle the consequences of coming out. They have heard similar stories of people being disowned and losing their jobs, and they decide it is too big a price to pay. Some of those homosexuals end up feeling trapped between their inner selves which are gay (and craving fresh air) and the exterior world which continually rewards them for not being gay. Unable to feel comfortable with either choice, they choose death, the final solution. Others tolerate the lies because they want the security of family and steady employment. However, they are so afraid of discovery that they choose anonymous sex partners off the street and end up a two-paragraph item in the morning newspaper: "Episcopal priest found naked and bound in bedroom, bludgeoned to death by hammer. No known suspects."

Coming out is a subject of great controversy. In a recent editorial in the *Advocate* newspaper, David Goodstein strongly, and I think harshly, attacks gay people in the closet. He seems ready to push people whether or not they are prepared.

In the past, I have said that people must be allowed to come out of the closet at their own pace. While I still believe that, I think the advice needs modifying. It is cruel and dangerous to throw a reluctant nonswimmer into a pool. Likewise, it is totally ineffective to suggest from a distance that they try it "only if they want to." The option, I think, is for the veteran swimmer to stand in the water with arms outstretched and to continually encourage the person at the side to try the water. "It's safe and it's invigorating." Why would anyone who doesn't swim jump into water without hearing why it's worth the experience and without some assurance he or she won't drown?

Michael, if you're alive, I'm in the pool and the water is

wonderful! I promise you that I never felt fully alive until I made the plunge. If you're gay, you're a natural swimmer. It's an essential aspect of being Michael.

When I jumped in the water, I lost all of the security I had on dry land. For a while, it was a security I didn't feel I could live without. But here I am—happy, well-integrated, growing in a wonderful relationship, the object of affection of previously frightened family and friends. I don't have much money but I have something money can't buy—integrity. I no longer fear being discovered. I no longer laugh at "fag" jokes. I don't worry about the mail carrier seeing "gay" on a return envelope, the bank clerk seeing "gay" on a check or the readers of the morning newspaper seeing "avowed homosexual" after my name.

More importantly, I have discovered wonderful things about myself. Some people may scoff at the generalizations, but I have witnessed a sensitivity in me and my gay friends that I have not found in most straight men. I have been freed of role playing too. In other words, I can take bows for my cooking, open doors for men and women, check the oil in my car without ever sensing that any of these activities are inappropriate. That's very liberating.

Affirming my homosexuality has enabled me to be the confidant of friends who now feel they can be honest about themselves without fearing judgment. It doesn't matter whether their issue is being fat, impotent, alcoholic or unfaithful. They now feel comfortable laying it out, shedding some tears and knowing that I can plug into their pain.

There's something about coming out which enables you to be authentic in many seemingly unrelated areas of life. That first important step toward self takes you out of the clutches of the world and its expectations. Your spiritual life, work life and social life become honest. Games are for people who can't be themselves.

If you jump into the pool, you may swallow some water. You may lose your balance and even momentarily be disoriented. That's part of the birthing process. All real growth involves some pain. But here I am, waiting to grab you, wanting to help you take that first stroke.

Don't jump into the pool unless there is a support system of some sort awaiting you. Don't leap from security unless you can be assured your immediate survival is possible. But don't stay on the sidelines too long. The sidelines mean death one way or another.

OPPRESSING
OURSELVES

April 1985

A few years ago, I clipped an article about a study on why German Christians didn't stop Hitler. The findings of the study, which I periodically reread, haunt me as a homosexual and they confuse me.

Hans O. Tiefel, associate professor of religion at the College of William and Mary, was awarded a National Endowment for the Humanities to explore why German Christians did not oppose Nazism and the Holocaust. He presented two startling findings. Tiefel said that the basis of the failure was the intricate web of church and state in Germany. The two had been so closely tied throughout Germany's history that it was difficult for German Christians to distinguish between the demands of each.

"There is always a nationalistic trend in any church," said Tiefel, "because people are not only believers but they're also citizens. . . . When Hitler came and put an end to the Weimar Republic, he asserted what he called positive Christianity, to appeal to Christians of all kinds. In fact, this was a kind of nationalism, just a propaganda term and not Christianity at all."

To me, it sounds very familiar. Ronald Reagan, Jerry Falwell, Jesse Helms and their friends may not be our Hitlers but they are all attempting to replace the stars of the American flag with crosses, and those crosses often represent the burial grounds of minority people like me. I am thankful for the American Civil Liberties Union, People for the American Way, the National Gay and Lesbian Task Force, the Human Rights Campaign Fund and other similar groups to which my partner, Ray, and I contribute. Their work helps diminish the chances of a Hitler gaining total control. Nevertheless, I remain on guard.

The other significant finding of Tiefel frightens me far more and confuses me terribly. One of the major reasons that "decent" Christians never really took a stand on behalf of Jews, he said, was the latent dislike of Jews that was reflected in language.

"The Jews were classified by terms which set them off as alien in nature. They were, in effect, dropped from human status and thereby lost the protection of ethics and law. Their less than human status was reflected in dehumanizing language."

Fairy, fruit, queer, lezzie, faggot, dyke, queen, flit, cocksucker and poof are words which, I feel, set me off as alien in nature. They suggest less than human status and they dehumanize me. I also think they dehumanize you, regardless of who is using them.

Kids today play a game called "Smear the Queer." Little gay kids play the game too. "Faggot" is the most horrible thing a young boy can be called by his friends. Gay adults can use the word with hostility too. According to a survey I conducted for the city of Boston, 76 percent of the gay men and lesbians who responded to the questionnaire reported being verbally assaulted on the street because they were gay or lesbian. In many places, such as Houston, and certainly in the nation as a whole, gay men and lesbians have been "dropped from human status and thereby lost the protection of ethics and law."

The similarities between the status of Jews in Germany and the status of homosexuals in the United States haunts me. In the survey that I conducted, called The Boston Project, 24 percent of the respondents stated they had been physically assaulted because they were gay, 20 percent had experienced discrimination in employment, 21 percent had been subjected to vandalism because they were gay and 13 percent said they lost housing because they were a fairy, fruit, queer, lezzie, faggot, dyke, queen, flit, cocksucker, poof or whatever.

What really confuses me about these facts is the notion that we gay people might unknowingly be collaborating with the enemy. I do not like the word *faggot* and I don't use it. That's my business and my privilege. I believe that language betrays bias; that just as ethnic jokes create false images of people, such as the Polish, so too words like *queen* create false images not only for the general public but also for the person being called them.

I'm not confused about what I find to be healthy behavior in my home. For instance, friends are asked not to tell ethnic jokes when visiting us. Friends are also encouraged not to use pet names for me or for Ray which suggest we are not men. What they call themselves in their own home is their business. Or is it? That's what really confuses me.

I feel that much of what we call gay culture is oppressive. I think that what we call ourselves (i.e., faggot, dyke, queer, etc.) is oppressive and leads to oppressive behavior. I feel that gay male bitchiness is oppressive. I feel that gay male flightiness is oppressive. I feel that the tired, shallow conversations of many gay men are oppressive. I think that camp is oppressive. I think that the culture we claim as uniquely gay is more the deposits of a heterosexually polluted river, left upon the banks of history, than it is any real expression of what we are and where we are going.

Our culture seems to be a sad reaction to heterosexual oppression. They hate us, so we make them laugh and then they tolerate us. Our humor, bittersweet and often pathetic, self-deprecating and pessimistic, becomes our self-mocking means of survival. I think that this is unconsciously collaborating with the enemy and contributing to our being "dropped from human status and thereby [losing] the protection of ethics and law."

On the other hand, I could be all wet. These expressed views of mine could be, as some will argue, an unconscious collaboration with the enemy. I may oppress gay men and lesbians, without knowing it, by presenting a philosophy which is Uncle Tomism. Maybe I'm a house nigger who has succeeded because I'm politely midwestern. Perhaps I will never be truly liberated until I call myself a "faggot" and my lover "Mary

Jane." Perhaps the culture which we have produced is a true expression of the rich pathos which is unique to homosexuals.

It could be, but I don't think so. Yet, I'm not sure and I am therefore confused.

What I am not confused about is that self-hate is the number one enemy of gay men and lesbians. I am not confused about the fact that most gay people I have met, young and old, want to live peaceful loving lives in the company of a significant other. I am not confused about the effect coming to our home has upon many gay people who didn't believe it was possible to be happy. I'm not confused about the horrible alcoholism, drug addiction and suicide rates in our community. I am not confused about how beautiful gay men and lesbians can be when they quit letting the heterosexual and the homosexual worlds tell them who they are.

If you're as concerned about and confused by the role language has in our self-esteem and status in society, consider conducting an experiment. Some day soon, sit down with a couple of close friends and ask them to honestly tell you how they feel about being gay. Ask them to tell you how they feel when they are called "faggot," "queen," "queer," "dyke." Ask them if they would feel comfortable in a gay setting talking about their relationship with God. Ask them about their hopes for love and what they want out of life. Tell them honestly how you feel about all of the above.

If you have adopted bitchiness as a means of survival, or camp as an identity, just as an experiment try not to be Joan Collins for a week. Instead, try to be yourself and try to help other gay men and lesbians be themselves. Sometimes, we keep our friends so much on the defensive that they are afraid to reveal any of their weaknesses to us.

Just for a week, try not to use the terms *faggot* and *dyke*. Just as an experiment, try complimenting another gay person for his or her healthy self-image. Tell a gay couple you are proud of their relationship and tell a person who dares to believe in God that you respect him or her.

If none of this makes any of us feel better about being gay and better about being alive, then all we have lost is a week. If, however, we begin to feel a little better about this special gift from God we call "gay," then maybe we will have started to develop an image and a culture which more aptly captures our unique beauty and demands that society recognize us as fully human.

MORE PLUSES

April 1978

A speaking engagement in Canada necessitated my flying to Montreal in the overwhelming company of a large group of boisterous, beer-bellied, middle-aged, Boston Irish hockey fanatics. Before the Delta flight was twenty minutes in the air, I was already beginning to make mental apologies for being both Irish and a resident of Boston. My only saving grace was being gay. Straight camp has no comparison.

Too frequently, lesbians and gay men find it necessary to apologize to straight friends for some of the idiosyncrasies which are associated with being homosexual. This is not to say that I enjoy being on a plane when the cabin is filled with outrageously campy gay men. I am merely saying that every charge which is made against gay people can be made with equal cogency against the nongay.

Is there a popular magazine today which contains ads any less exploitative than those in gay publications? Is having a Colt model on the front cover of *Mandate* any more sexist than using Cheryl Tiegs to sell *Time* magazine? Is the alleged narcissism of the gay scene any different than that ritualized by John Travolta in front of his bedroom mirror in *Saturday Night Fever*?

Are gay pride parades any more "offensive" than the promenade on St. Patrick's Day in New York and Boston? Are gay motorcycle clubs any more caricatured than the Shriners? Is

Edith Bunker any better a representation of the "perfect woman" than the stereotypical "butch dyke"?

While I was in Canada, one woman commented that we spend too much time talking about what is wrong with the gay scene and not enough time accenting what is good about it. What is "good" and "bad" obviously is a matter of opinion, but I think she is right.

Gay people seem far more concerned about exploitation than nongays, if people are able to believe what they read in newspapers. Many gay publications deal daily with the threat of going under because they refuse to accept ads which are sexist.

Gay people who insist upon maintaining ties with their religious institutions provide us with the finest examples in modern history of martyrs for the faith. Who, besides lesbians and gay men are attempting to get into churches today?

Gay people tend to be far less sexist in language, attitudes and actions. As many complaints as we hear about bars which require women to have three pieces of I.D., there is a far greater effort on the part of gay men to eliminate language which defines all people under the category of "man." How frequently do we see the word *person* substituted in straight publications for the word *man* or *men* when the gender is unknown?

Gay people, as a whole, challenge the psychiatric profession as no other group of Americans has dared before by ignoring their "scientific" findings, thereby calling into question their credentials.

Gay people are pioneering in the area of relationships and sexual expression. With no or few role models to follow, lesbians and gay men have been forced to abandon preconceived notions of the meaning of relationship and by trial and error have discovered that the healthiest relationship is designed by the individuals involved.

Gay people are challenging definitions of what it means to be male and female. We are, again, discovering for ourselves what potential we have for doing things previously taboo for our genders.

By standing in defiance of near-universal condemnation and by surviving centuries of planned purges, lesbians and gay men offer other oppressed persons the hope of becoming their own persons.

To those persons who are victimized for sexual practices other than homosexual or heterosexual, the gay movement has offered a place where fears can be verbalized and hopes expressed. Bisexuals, transsexuals and transvestites are generally greeted with far more empathy than they would ever encounter in straight society.

While it goes without saying that there is much wrong with the general attitude toward the aged, blacks, the handicapped and all other persons who are externally different from the majority of gay people, none of these biases are peculiar to us. Moreover, an objective look suggests, I think, that we are struggling to eliminate the biases and prejudices we each picked up as children from the heterosexual media.

Sometimes it amazes me that any of us even survive the constant pressure we receive from nongays and from each other. Too often we take our survival for granted as if it was a matter of luck.

This essay is not an invitation to end our struggle to eliminate sexism, exploitation, agism, racism, classism, and all of the other evils which plague us as Americans, but more to encourage an occasional pat on the back that we have come as far as we have.

More than any other generation of homosexuals in the history of the world, we have the opportunity to make things a lot easier for those who follow us. More than the opportunity, we have the responsibility. Few persons will be aware of our struggle fifty years from now, any more than we can imagine life without electricity. But the simple knowledge that the little ones who grow up knowing they're gay won't be forced to hide their light under a bushel should be enough cause for celebration today. Perhaps our liberation will have its effect upon nongays too, so that young straight children will not have to be embarrassed by their parents while accompanying them to a hockey game in Montreal.

THE NEXT STEP

November 1980

A woman appearing on a morning talk show recently was introduced as a transsexual priest. She sat comfortably as the host probed into her past, but finally concluded she didn't know why she was appearing on his show. The comment, at first, seemed terribly naive. Surely she was there to make people comfortable with transgender identity. What's more, she's the perfect person to test the Catholic Church's ban on ordaining women to the priesthood. But she didn't say that.

Later, I realized what a terrific statement she was making by not needing to make any statement at all. While she said she was indeed concerned about women's rights and the needs of other transsexuals, she wasn't on television to prove anything to anybody. She had hoped she was invited to discuss her study of reincarnation.

What a beautiful message: She liked herself. While her story is fascinating, her statement is profound. This woman is comfortable with herself and doesn't plan to spend the rest of her life explaining her transsexualism.

I would like to think that is the next evolutionary step for gay men and women: that rather than spend our lives defending ourselves to family, friends and working cohorts, we get about the business of being ourselves, enjoying life and putting our homosexuality into proper perspective.

It is an albatross around the neck of most minority people that we feel we must constantly prove ourselves. We stand before the viewing majority and insist through a variety of ways that we are just as reliable, just as decent, just as patriotic, just as religious, just as masculine and feminine, just as normal.

In years past, I, as a white person, have watched black friends straighten their hair, struggle with word pronunciation different from their own and worship in a style which for them lacked meaning. As a man, I have painfully witnessed women friends reject help on the highway, scoff at an opened door and refuse a warm smile. As a Christian, I have been torn by news of Jews feeling the need to change their last names or assemble Christmas lights securely around their front doors.

Being a homosexual, I, too, have felt the need to project an image. I am careful to refrain from public displays of affection, from leaving *Blueboys* in sight of visiting relatives, from being the least bit "effeminate" in front of straight audiences. I have friends who mess up the bed in the guest room so the maid won't know they're gay; who are afraid to subscribe to a gay publication for fear of what the mail carrier might think; who have moved across the country so their families will never know of their activities and friends.

In other words, many of us are living our lives to prove we are or we're not what even strangers might imagine; strangers who probably couldn't care less. I don't think it's healthy.

I don't want my black friends to be white. I don't want my women friends to be men. I don't want my Jewish friends to be Christian. Their uniqueness is part of what I find attractive. If their differences make me uncomfortable, it's my responsibility to adjust. Why then am I so hard on myself when it comes to my differences? Why am I so preoccupied with my homosexuality and the effect it might have on others?

Sometimes I wonder how much of my life is an attempt to prove to my folks that they didn't fail. How much of my life is an attempt to prove to the Church that I am still worthy of its praise? How much of what I do for a living is an attempt to prove to myself that I'm okay?

I want to be freed up of the need to prove anything to anybody. I want to live without expectations and images. I want to let go of the "shoulds" and begin focusing on the "wants" and "needs."

What does it require to make such a significant evolutionary step? What does the process of letting go demand of us? In the November issue of *Psychology Today* there is a good article about the need to be perfect and the toll it takes. Troubled personal relationships, impaired health, low self-esteem and depression are the potential results of attempting to be something you cannot be, according to the author. We gay people who attempt to be perfectly gay or perfectly straight in the world invite anxiety and exhaustion.

Modified for our purposes, the advice given to perfectionists seems most appropriate. We are encouraged to begin by making a list of all the advantages and disadvantages of living to meet other people's expectations. Where's the payoff? Second, we should determine how much satisfaction we think we will get by playing a role and then play the role to see how much satisfaction we actually received. Another technique is to keep track during the day with a list of the times we compromised ourselves. Why did we do it and what were the results? Eventually, the perfectionist or the person who lives a role will let go of expectations and learn that being average or being yourself is far more comfortable.

That's what I want to be: an average guy who happens to be gay, and, like the woman who happens to be a transsexual priest, feel I have nothing to prove.

LIVING FOR
YOURSELF

March 1986

In therapy, recently, I have been nervously probing a new dimension of involvement in life. With my patient and caring guide, I have been exploring the possibility that there is yet another Brian emerging.

For the last several years, it has seemed clear to me that there have been at least two Brian McNaughts in my history. There was, and is, the ever-perfect altar boy who thrived on strokes, sought to please and hid in fright his desire to sleep with Tarzan. He was, and is, like many other gay men I know, "the best little boy in the world," as the title of the popular book suggests. The first Brian was born to Waldo and Virginia in Detroit, Michigan, in 1948. Twenty-six years later, Desperation and Hope gave birth to a second Brian whose entry into the world was publicly announced as a "coming out." Still prone to thrive on strokes and seek to please, the new Brian no longer hid his desire to sleep with Tarzan, actor Robert Conrad or the priest with whom he was living.

Confident, courageous and guided by a dream of a world in which young gay kids could safely walk hand in hand alongside of young straight kids, the new Brian was also frightened, defensive and troubled by feelings of disconnectedness from those important persons, places and things of his former life in the closet. He insisted that he loved everything about the past except for the lies, but he felt that he was no longer loved by everyone from the past.

It seemed to the new Brian that most people felt that there had indeed been a birth of a new person and that tragically the old Brian was dead. The new Brian wasn't the boy they knew. He was a stranger. But the new Brian protested that he was the very same person. Didn't he still love his family? Didn't he still love his Church? Didn't he still feel guilty about masturbating? The only thing new about him, he insisted, was his unwillingness to lie anymore about himself. He was gay. He had always been gay. He assured everyone, particularly himself, that, beyond that, he was still the same person. Yet, no one seemed convinced, except Brian.

With time, however, it became clear even to Brian that he wasn't the same person. He was very different. The first Brian was a whimp, it was eventually decided by the second. The second Brian was not. The first Brian was an embarrassment to the second for having spent so much time and expended so much energy attempting to convince himself and everyone else that he was a heterosexual.

The old Brian spent many, many years in the confessional feeling guilty about being a homosexual. The second Brian spent many, many years in therapy feeling angry about previously feeling so guilty. The Brian who seems to be emerging is not only not guilty but he is not so angry anymore either. His parents seem to be Dissatisfaction and Curiosity. This new Brian is tired of living in reaction to the world and excited about better understanding his place in life. He seems to be much less defensive, much less alienated from his past than the second Brian. This all feels good. What doesn't feel really comfortable is that the newest Brian doesn't yet know what changing his perspective will do to his life.

Having spent nearly one third of his existence writing, preaching, acting, dreaming, organizing, breathing about life as a gay man whose sole focus was reacting to and eliminating all homophobia from the face of the world, the new, emerging Brian feels quite frightened about broadening his focus. "If I don't do what I have always done in the same way I have always done it," he nervously asks his gay therapist, "what do I do?"

"What do you want to do?" the therapist midwife asks the infant. Sometimes I want to go running back into my shell because it is there that I am comfortable. I am comfortable being angry about the injustices I face as a gay man. I am comfortable feeling oppressed. After all of these years I have finally established a niche for myself. My friends know what I am about. My parents know what I am about. I have given up so much to be where I am today.

"But what is it that you want to do?" I want to laugh at myself more. I want to let go of some of my agenda so that I have more time to experience life as it comes. I want to be exempted from always checking our friends' refrigerators to ensure that they did not buy Coors. I want to be able to watch television shows about homosexuality without waiting like a hawk for the politically incorrect line. I want not to feel guilty because I don't read every issue of *Newsweek* or watch every segment of "Donahue" that pertains to homosexuality. I want to unclench my fists a little.

"But what is that you want to do?" continues my patient guide. "You keep telling me what you don't want." I'm not sure. I just have this feeling inside of me that there is something more out there. I have the feeling that I don't yet know myself as a gay person. I know myself as a little boy who pretended to be straight because he was afraid of not being loved. I know myself as an adult who publicly affirmed his homosexuality but spent all of his time reacting defensively to what others said about him. But what if I quit responding like Pavlov's dog to straight expectations and began spending my time and energy attempting to better understand what it is that makes me special; what it is that makes me different? I'm halfway through my life and I want to spend the rest of it freely and creatively nurturing my full development.

According to one model of development, my probing of a new dimension of involvement in life is predictable and healthy. Liberation is a five-part process which begins in a stage called "Being." Here we have no knowledge of our being different from other people. Soon, however, innocence ends and we enter the "Swallowing" stage, during which we learn through a variety of means that there is something different about us which makes us unacceptable to the rest of society. We believe the message we hear—that homosexual feelings equal sinfulness, sickness and sadness—because we are hearing it from people we trust. To compensate and to survive, most of us fight our feelings and we work hard to win the approval of those people we fear and admire most—heterosexuals.

When we can no longer deny we are gay and can no longer stand silent about the lies we were told and had swallowed, we come out of the closet and enter the "Separating" stage. It is here that we assert ourselves as gay gladiators and do battle with the attitudes of family, the Church, lawmakers, the press and others who say bad things about being gay. Our life's agenda is to react to all forms of gay oppression. When straight people say that gay men are sissies, we prove to them that we are not. When straight people say that gay people are outside of God's plan, we prove to them that we can be better Catholics, Protestants and Jews than they can. "Give us your best shot," we tell them as we continue to work hard to win the approval of those we fear and admire most—heterosexuals.

What happens next is what I seem to be experiencing. When we tire of reacting to straight people and their expectations, or even to the expectations of other gay people, we enter the next stage which is called "Building." In this stage we quit reacting and begin acting; we quit responding and begin questioning for ourselves: "What is it that makes me as a gay person special? What is gay masculinity or femininity? What is gay spirituality? What gifts do I have to offer because of my homosexuality? Who do I and should I admire most?"

There is another stage. It is called "Extending." Once we have learned for ourselves the strengths and weaknesses of who we are and have determined for ourselves what will make us happy, we are then able to respond freely to all of the other persons, gay or straight, who have also gone through or are caught in the stages of Being, Swallowing, Separating, Building and Extending.

Like all growth, leaving one stage for another is not a painless process nor is it one which happens all at once. It is a gradual emergence. In this stage of "Building" I find that I do not care less about my liberation and that of every other gay man or lesbian, but I see the battle for me in a different arena than it has been. I see my preoccupation with the expectations and the actions of heterosexuals as far more my enemy than they themselves are. I want to go to my grave knowing not that I have persuaded one or more generations of heterosexual Americans that I am a decent human being but rather knowing that I have spent at least half of my life living free of someone else's expectations and that I have died as a gay man who fully understood, appreciated and celebrated his homosexuality. That's a tough task but the sooner I focus on it instead of on what I want others to believe, the better the chance I have of seeing it happen.

A CELEBRATION
OF SELF

August 1985

The conference room was dark, like a closet. In the many chairs along the outer perimeter sat a semicircle of heterosexuals or those who wished to be thought of as such. In front of them, equally spaced in the same semicircle, stood five gay men holding unlit candles. We were Joe, Jerry, Bob, Brian and Michael.

I am what I am
I am my own special creation.
So, come take a look,
give me the hook or the ovation.

George Hearn's voice of controlled indignation and pride filled the room with the gay and lesbian anthem from a recording of *La Cage Aux Folles*. Joe lit his candle and stretched it out with a straight arm in front of him, like a fearless guide leading the lost through an abyss.

Joe is in his fifties, the eldest of our group. He came to this week-long sexuality conference for teachers, ministers, counselors, youth workers and others as an alleged heterosexual. He had been in a twenty-year relationship before his lover died eight years ago. Then he spent seven years locked up in his apartment, alone and afraid of loneliness. Now, he was out in the world again and he wanted to be thought of as a professional, particularly by those others at the conference from his hometown who knew him only as a college professor. Joe had never participated in any event which called attention to, let alone celebrated, his homosexuality. When I proposed to the gay men (no lesbians were present) that we participate as a group in the conference's last night of "Celebration," they all agreed with varying degrees of enthusiasm. Joe was frightened but determined to take advantage of the atmosphere of acceptance which seemed to have developed among the straight participants. His candle broke his silence.

It's my world that I want to have
a little pride in;
My world, and it's not a place
I have to hide in.

Jerry was the youngest and the newest to the concept that being gay was a gift to celebrate. This twenty-five-year-old courageously told the entire group on the first day that he was gay and said that he was struggling with it. He was not comfortable.

As most of the heterosexuals present, Jerry was ill at ease as we watched sexually explicit films on male and female homosexuality. He said that he was attracted to the men in the film as he had been to men his whole life, but he thought it was wrong. We went for a long walk after my presentation on homosexuality to the conferees, and Jerry described what he feared about being gay. Only "out" to himself for three months, he feared that if he really accepted his homosexuality, he would have to change; he would have to become a different Jerry, a Jerry who wouldn't recognize his former, decent, fun-loving, ethical self. Being gay, he was convinced, meant being promiscuous; being lonely; being drunk; being immoral; being divorced from the things which had, to date, given his life meaning.

In the beginning, Jerry seemed enthusiastic about participating as a group of gay men in the celebration, but shortly before the evening's program began, he told us that he would sit it out. "I just don't believe what we're saying," he pleaded. Yet, during the skits, songs and poetry readings by other participants that night, Jerry stared at the floor seemingly lost and ashamed. During a break, I asked the master of ceremonies to plan on a five-minute recess before we gay men began our presentation. I then sought out Jerry to say that whatever he decided to do was okay and that there would be time to change his mind if he wanted to be a part of the group.

The second candle lit was Jerry's. He held it in his left hand. His right arm was around the shoulder of a woman friend upon whom he leaned for critical support.

> *I am what I am*
> *I don't want praise, I don't want pity.*
> *I bang my own drum*
> *Some think it's noise, I think it's pretty.*

Next came Bob. Thirty years old and ready to pounce on the world like a puppy let off its leash for the first time, Bob bloomed at the conference in a way that makes the heart of a gay activist burst with pride. He walked on air as he privately confided, "I'm going home to my parish and I'm coming out to everyone. I want to start talking to groups about being gay like Brian does. I feel so connected." I saw myself as I watched him soar to emotional heights he had never thought possible. I did, however, do my best to temper with reason his plans to immediately embark upon the career of gay activist.

> *Your life is a sham*
> *'til you can shout out loud*
> *"I am what I am"*

My candle was next. I was shaking so with pride for Bob and Joe that it took me two tries to light the wick. When I finally did succeed, I illuminated eyes which were puffy with tears over the sight of Jerry standing tall to my left.

> *I am what I am*
> *and what I am needs no excuses*

I deal my own deck
sometimes the ace, sometimes the deuces.

It's one life
and there's no return and no deposit;
one life
so it's time to open up your closet.

Life's not worth a damn
'til you can say
"Hey world, I am what I am."

Michael was the last in the large semicircle to light his candle. He, like me, has been out for at least ten years and, like me, is a "recovering perfect person." A best little boy in the family and in the church, Michael is now dealing with his anger at the injustices in his life and he is proudly and confidently claiming space in the world as his own. He is a mature gay man who lives not in reaction to straight people but rather in response to the invitation of life to grow to his full potential.

As the song ended, we took turns reading short passages from lesbian and gay authors about the experience of being gay. As we finished our reading, we walked slowly to the center of the room and encircled an oblong box on the floor. When Michael joined the circle, the lights were turned on, the recording of "I Am What I Am" was replayed and the box was opened to reveal several dozen white sweetheart roses. These we took and ceremoniously handed a rose, accompanied by a good, long hug, to each nongay participant.

Our plan was then to regroup in the center of the room, await the song's conclusion and exit to the thunderous applause. However, when we finished handing out our roses and hugs, we realized that everyone in the room was weeping and hugging one another. Joe, Jerry, Bob, Michael and I then began hugging each other and eventually ended up in one intergenerational embrace of affirmation.

"Thank you for allowing me to be honest for the first time in my life," whispered Joe. "I'm so proud and I'm so happy."

"Unreal," gasped Bob. "This is unreal. Look at those people hug and cry. Dammit we did it. We really did it. I will never forget this as long as I live."

"How you doing?" I asked Michael as we held onto each other for dear life.

"I'm great. I'm just great."

"How's Jerry?" I asked.

"Hey, Jerry, how are you doing?" we asked together.

Jerry smiled coyly. "Piece of cake."

GROWING UP
GAY

GROWING UP
GAY

A good friend once commented that the most awful thing about being gay is forgetting how awful it *was*. Too frequently, once we have come out and established a comfortable niche for ourselves, we forget the pain we felt as isolated persons in school and in the family. This process of forgetting puts us out of touch with those young gay people who follow us in time. Growing up gay in high school and college today is no small task. Some people just barely make it. The stories which come out of the struggle for survival are often heroic tales of daring: Gay people daring to accept the unacceptable; daring to step forward in defense of themselves; daring to risk even the loss of their family's love in their struggle for self-acceptance. One day you are enough in charge of your life to say boldly, "Hey, world, I like myself," and mean it. But getting to that point is no easy trek.

HIGH SCHOOL
HORRORS

1981

Perhaps the saddest letter I have received from a gay person in the last several years arrived recently and was signed "A Friend?" The handwritten note was in response to a column of mine on learning to overcome the fear of violence.

"I'm glad to know other people were afraid too," wrote the young man. "You said you didn't consider yourself a 'sissy' (in high school). I didn't have the choice; it was drummed into me every day of every school year for 12 years. I was a loving, caring person inside but no one looked beyond the way I carried my books and the way I talked.

"They broke me long before my high school graduation and helped to mold me into a very shy and utterly alone human being who needs three drinks now just to get up enough nerve to say 'Hi' to someone in the bar. I'm so afraid of people—just terrified."

That letter, along with a book called *Reflections of a Rock Lobster*, by Aaron Fricke, and a couple of therapy sessions have put me more in touch with the enormous private pain I experienced in high school as a confused, closeted gay adolescent and the price I paid for survival. They also energized my desire to help make things easier for those who now struggle for their emotional lives in our tax-supported schools.

Spend a minute with me, if you will, reflecting on the four years we spent in high school. Forget the security we feel today and remember the pretending, the fear of being discovered, the isolation and the agony of doubt we felt as fourteen, fifteen, sixteen, and seventeen-year-olds. Do you recall the "fag" jokes and everybody (including us) calling each other "queer"? Do you remember the graffiti on the john walls and how we thought it was meant for us? Do you recall the paranoia we felt in gym class—most especially in the showers? Were we successful in finding a book in the library or a pamphlet outside of the guidance office which would help us understand our feelings? Did we even dare look? Do you remember classmates like the guy who wrote the letter—the boys who "held their books like a girl" and the girls "who walked like a boy"? Did we call them "queer," "faggot," "dyke" behind their backs because we wanted to be part of the crowd and we feared being labeled ourselves? I remember all of that and more.

From therapy, I am learning about the elaborate defense mechanisms I established to protect myself and about the many days I agonized over what would happen to me if I revealed my fantasies. I was positive I would be ostracized and would lose the love of everyone of importance to me. When I finally did come out and, indeed, lost job, family and friends, my defense mechanisms were reinforced. Today, I struggle with a lack of trust not unlike that expressed by the young man who says he's "afraid of people." I curse the process which created such a shell.

A lot has changed since I was in high school. Aaron Fricke, the young man who went to the Cumberland, Rhode Island, senior prom with a male date, represents a new generation of gay youth. His book speaks of pride, courage and open struggle, and, in that, it is heartening. But it also speaks of terror—of kids throwing disected animals at him in biology class because he was suspected of being gay; of classmates spattering his clothes with spit during study hall, punching him in the hallway and writing graffiti on his parent's home in the dark of night. While today's gay and lesbian youth are more sure of their sexual identity, are coming out sooner and with more enthusiasm than people of my generation did, they are also suffering a higher degree of intolerance from their peers in school because of the expected backlash to the gay civil rights movement.

I suggest that we have an enormous responsibility to the gay adolescents who follow us. Our hard work as gay adults fighting for our civil rights is making it easier for gay high school students to develop a positive gay identity, but we are also creating an atmosphere of hysteria which is far more threatening for them than what we encountered. We can't afford to sit back and wait with open arms for them to leave the high school situation. I feel we have to concentrate more of our efforts on protecting them today before too great a toll is taken. How do we do that?

Much of my work is with high school sex educators. They tell me that only 10 percent of the nation's high schools have anything resembling a sex education program and that even in many of these schools, talking about homosexuality is generally forbidden. This is the result of the efforts of a small number of parents who protest to school boards and principals and intimidate them into compliance. (These principals, it should be remembered, are paid salaries out of our tax dollars.) One way of making sure that gay and nongay students get a healthy understanding of homosexuality is for adult gay members of the community to have their strong voices heard in the schools, before principals and at school board meetings. We have to insist that homosexuality be discussed.

A simple and direct means of accomplishing this is for us to contact the principal or guidance office of our alma mater. When I received a recent request for money from my high school, I wrote the principal and reminded him that when I was a senior, the guidance counselor told us he would kick us out of his office if we told him we were "queer." I asked him what the policy of the school was today and I also inquired whether he would be willing to place a copy of my book, *A Disturbed Peace*, in the school library. Not every response will be as supportive as his. To my delight, he said he would be "proud" to have a copy of the book available to students and added, ". . . you are writing and speaking with great conviction about something which many, many people would shy away from despite what they thought. I admire you a lot."

Even if your inquiry is not as well received, every letter sent will effectively raise the consciousness of the school's administration. High schools which do not offer a supportive environment for gay and lesbian students should be deprived of gay alumni funds. The opposite is also true. Support should be rewarded. Likewise, contributions of gay-oriented books for the school library are an important means of providing help to gay students. We should be prepared, however, to fight to keep those books on the shelves when one or two parents attempt to remove them.

Regarding pamphlets, *20 Questions About Homosexuality*, published by the National Gay and Lesbian Task Force, is one booklet I feel would be a welcomed addition to any guidance office rack. Perhaps you know of others. If the guidance department says they would like to have such pamphlets but the money is not in the budget, consider buying them yourself as your contribution to the movement. If one gay student reads the pamphlet and is comforted, our gift is invaluable.

Finally, in many cities in the country, there are organizations for gay and lesbian youth. They need financial and moral support. We can learn a great deal from these young people about their fears, hopes and trials and can perhaps, therefore, see how we might better direct our energies.

Our common experience of oppression is one of the strongest links we have as a community. We can't afford to forget our pain. Nor can we forget that alienation, intimidation and isolation continue to pollute the lives of those who follow in our footsteps. It would seem that those of us who have suffered and survived are the ones who should be sensitive enough and courageous enough to address the issue.

THE PROM

June 1980

High school junior and senior proms across the country this spring were undoubtedly dominated by the scene of tuxedoed halfbacks mockingly tapping the shoulders of their male buddies to ask for a dance. That's all right, guys. Have your fun. Laughter helps ease anxiety. But there is history being made and you're part of it. The rights of gay people have taken a giant leap forward and I couldn't be happier. A U.S. district court in Rhode Island recently ruled that to deny permission to an eighteen-year-old senior to take a male escort to the school prom would be a violation of the student's constitutional right of free association. With blackened eye and undoubtedly an upset stomach, Aaron Fricke took Paul Guilbert to the Cumberland, Rhode Island, high school senior prom. Fricke wasn't the first to attend a school prom as a male-escorted gay student, but he was the first to have the support of the courts.

Last year at this time, when Paul Guilbert was denied permission by the same school to attend the event with a male date, I wished out loud for the day when I could chaperone a school prom at which gay couples danced with as much abandon as their straight classmates. Like a parent who endured the Depression, I want those who follow my generation to have more than we did and to be spared unnecessary suffering. The thought of gay high school students being affirmed enough to identify themselves as gay; the thought of them being able to ask a person of their choice to a school function, to be free of the pressure to lie and conform, to laugh at the ignorance of the rest of the world, makes my heart dance.

Had I been liberated enough at eighteen to ask a male date to my prom and had the world been liberated enough to permit it, I think I would have dared to ask Peter Murray to be my date. Peter was the most handsome man I had ever seen. A transfer student, he had the nicest smile, best body and hairiest chest in school. I don't know that he was gay. I didn't even know that anyone was homosexual besides me and even that I couldn't verbalize. But if I had the chance to do it over again, Aaron and Paul having broken the ice, I would probably ask Peter.

Like every gay person I know, I went to the prom with a "friend." Her name was Martha Bloom. She was a girl with a great sense of humor whom I dated through most of high school. We laughed a lot.

As was the tradition, I borrowed Dad's car for the occasion. I spent lots of money renting a white tuxedo and buying Martha's gardenia. Martha, too, spent lots of money. She bought an expensive gown and had her hair done. She looked great and beamed with excitement over dinner and at the country club. For Martha, this was the magic night to which she had looked forward since she entered high school. The senior prom—the most romantic event in a young woman's life: fancy new dress, orchestra music, no curfew. Her mind swam with expectations.

Martha closed her eyes as we danced. I stretched my neck to watch Peter. Wasn't he handsome? Didn't he look sharp? I wonder if he's having a good time?

I didn't fantasize dancing with Peter. Such a thought was beyond my imagination. I thought more about how I wished we were sitting at the same table and going to the same afterparty. I thought how I wished we were close friends, buddies, back-slapping chums.

As the evening drew to a close, I watched the different couples dance slower and closer, slower and closer. The women began running their fingers up and down their dates' backs. The guys nestled their noses into the napes of the girls' necks and tenderly kissed them. Martha held me tight and stroked my back. I cracked a joke and made her laugh. Laughter helps ease anxiety.

That was yesterday. Today is different. Fourteen years later, two men in Cumberland, Rhode Island, danced together at their school's senior prom. The price they paid (and will continue to pay) was enormous. They undoubtedly spent the night keeping each other laughing. They may not have had any fun. But they went and the American judicial system said they had the right to go. Senior proms will never be the same again.

That was today. Tomorrow will be different. Tomorrow young gay men and women will decide whether they want to go to the prom. If they do, they will select the partner of their choice. If they rent a tux or buy a gown, they will do so with excitement. They won't need to stare with pain across the dance floor. They won't have to laugh their way through the last song.

Thank you, Aaron. Thank you, Paul.

♦

COURAGE
ON CAMPUS

May 1985

The big, black, bold lettering on the hand-printed poster declared: HETEROSEXUALS FIGHT BACK!! Copies were hung on billboards, trees and telephone poles throughout the sprawling university campus.

"Protest Friday's 'Hug a Homosexual' Booth," it summoned. "Join us in a march . . . to the Student Union. Once there we will hang a dummy representing the Gay/Lesbian movement. THIS IS NOT A JOKE!!"

We didn't have a gay movement to protest against when I was in school in the late 1960s, but had that threatening declaration appeared on the walls of my dorm or fraternity house, I'm afraid I might have sought sanctuary in church, in a six-pack or in the march itself. I have changed, as have the times, yet, college campuses, which I visit regularly as a speaker, continue to arouse in me that irritating fear of straight white male jocks I have had since youth.

Actually, it's not the men themselves I fear but the totally irrational behavior of which they are capable. Perhaps it's the testosterone hormones in wild flux which can make so many sixteen-to-twenty-one-year-old men such unpredictable and often cruel adolescents, but college years can be a rite of passage during which manhood is often proven by how many times you can throw up and keep drinking, how many virgins you can deflower and how many homosexuals you can intimidate.

A great deal has changed since the turbulent, closeted days of unrest on college campuses in the late 1960s. Today, nearly every college has an active and growing gay and lesbian student group; nearly every collegiate library has at least a few good books on being gay that you can check out without the librarian being needed to unlock a "restricted" cage and many campus counseling centers and campus ministers are more open to and supportive of gay men and lesbians. However, college fraternities and male dorms continue to house human beings capable of primitive animal behavior, like urinating on the door of a suspected homosexual. It is important to keep that in mind as we unfold the story of John Jablonski, a senior at a local university and president of its gay and lesbian student group.

The effect of the "Heterosexuals Fight Back" poster was predictable. John watched as his group's members wrestled with anxious questions like "Who are these heterosexuals who want to fight back? How many will march? What will they do? What should we do?" Undoubtedly, given our own learned homophobia, some of them probably privately thought "It's our own fault. We've asked for too much. We should have kept a lower profile. They are probably sick of hearing us talk about it."

The male student who instigated the march against the gay and lesbian group bragged about it around campus, so it wasn't hard for John to discover who was behind the measure. Several options were open to him and the group. They could approach the dean of students or another university official and seek to have the march stopped and the student disciplined. They could attempt to use the incident as an educational tool and secure the support of other groups on campus, like those for women and for people of color. They could petition the student government or solicit sympathy from the staff of the student newspaper. They could cancel their "Hug a Homosexual" booth and maintain a low profile for the next several weeks. They could also seek sanctuary in the church, a six-pack or in the march itself.

As the group pondered its options, John Jablonski decided on an approach he needed to take himself. John decided to talk one on one (he thought) with the man who planned to hang a dummy representing the Gay/Lesbian movement. After dinner one evening he walked by himself into the colosseum, the student dormitory on the other side of campus, which housed the heterosexual "militant" and his friends.

When he finally found the student's room, there was no one there. The man in question, he was told, might be in another room on the floor where some students were having a party. Led by the sound of boisterous laughter, John found a roomful of men, presumably all straight and presumably all potential marchers in the antigay parade.

"Hi, I'm John Jablonski," he interrupted. "I'm president of the Gay and Lesbian Student Group. I'm looking for . . ." he explained to the now silent room. The man in question wasn't there but he was expected. The others, however, amused and taken aback by his audacity, encouraged John to stay and began to ask him questions. He answered them directly, one by one, as he stood in his coat and leaned against the door.

The number of people in the room fluctuated between eight and twenty, with the size not decreasing because of John's presence but increasing. Each question led to another and another. Student after student walked by John into the room. Finally, the sponsor of the antigay march appeared.

"Hi, I'm John Jablonski," he explained in the hushed room, his arm outstretched. "I'm president of the Gay and Lesbian Student Group and I came over to talk with you about your planned march. I wanted you to know how it is affecting me and the others in the group."

Initially hostile and indignant, the male student sought the approval of his buddies in the room. He didn't get it. "Listen to what he has to say," his friends encouraged.

John proceded to explain what it was like to be gay on that campus and in general. He explained what the student group was all about and how the "Hug a Homosexual" booth was an attempt to educate people. He told how hurtful and frightening the posters were and how threatening the march could be to people who were struggling to feel good about themselves. He asked that the anti-gay march be canceled.

The group and the sponsor listened carefully. Finally, after spending a couple of hours together, the man who hand-printed the big, black, bold lettering HETEROSEXUALS FIGHT BACK explained that to save face he would have to go through with the march but said that he was sorry. He said that he now better understood what gay liberation was all about.

When John Jablonski left that college dorm room, he was enthusiastically applauded by the straight men who had assembled there. They applauded his courage and his honesty. All of them went back to their rooms having met at least one self-affirmed homosexual. They may not have suddenly decided to approve of homosexuality or even to support the fight for gay and lesbian rights, but they were changed men to some degree and they weren't about to march across campus to protest gay people, at least not to protest John Jablonski being who he was.

The day of the march, only three people walked across campus and they did so silently. The sponsor of the protest then issued a public apology for his actions. I don't know how many people showed up to "Hug a Homosexual," but I can think of one guy who deserved a big hug.

CLASS REUNION

May 1980

The invitation to the tenth anniversary of my college graduation was signed "Fondly, Charlene." The woman I nearly married
now lives with her family on Pelican Lane in Wisconsin.

My dark side imagined Pelican Lane being dominated by
turquoise houses on postage stamp lots adorned with pink
flamingoes and shrines to Mary. A subsequent letter from
Charlene was printed on notepaper which depicted her 100-
year-old farm on five acres of Pelican Lane. It carried a snapshot
of two adorable children and her handsome husband, a former
fraternity brother whom I secretly hoped had gained 200
pounds per year since we left Marquette.

I wrote back that I would love to go to the reunion were it
not for the expense of travel. I lied. At this point in my development, I don't want to return to my past; I'm not ready. I feel I
have come too far to return to the place where I protested
against all of society's injustices except my own. Returning to
Milwaukee to see the men and women with whom I shared four
significant years of my life would be an unnecessary confrontation with the unresolved pain of my experiences there. The invitation alone had already begun the process.

Some gay people have told me they breezed through college. It was a dream, they say. They went to bars; they were
"out." A few even state they had a lover for a roommate! Not

me. For me and for a lot of others it was a nightmare. Too often, I think, we gay people who survived the nightmare and who have built ourselves a happy and fulfilling life allow ourselves to forget how dreadful the past has been. In so doing, we cut ourselves off from the pain which continues in the lives of those who followed us into high school, the army or college.

At a ten-year reunion I know I would encounter straight peers who would laughingly reminisce about their terror of failing Mark Highland's ethics class or about the time they broke curfew and were grounded during the basketball championships. But I would want to talk about how many times I thought of ending my life because of the "monster" that was growing inside. I would want to talk about how alone I felt in the midst of their laughter.

I remember my college years as an ordeal rather than an opportunity. That's not to say I didn't have fun in college. It was at Marquette that I learned to drink beer and to stay up all night playing bridge. But as was true for most gay men and women I know, college was more significantly a frightening and insecure time dominated by self-hate, pretending and paranoiac reacting.

Were I to return to Milwaukee, I fear I would be confronted with the memories of a Brian I barely recognize; a Brian whose anguish continues to anger me and whose awkwardness I have tried to forget. Held securely in the memory of others, he was a man who the women murmured was unattainable. Intensely religious, highly energetic, anxious to please, he was a puzzle unsolved even by himself. His sophomore year he cooperated in the purging of the fraternity pledgemaster who was accused of being "queer." As a junior he fumbled through a homosexual encounter in the dorm and spent the next two years dreaming about the man at night and avoiding him during the day. As a senior, with only one such experience under his belt, he achieved peace by promising he would never sleep with a man he liked.

That's my history at Marquette and while I'm curious whether Pat ever got a job, Pam ever confronted her mother and Paulette ever straightened out John, my need at a reunion would be to pull people into the past and confront them with my unresolved anguish. Only then would the women know why I never kissed them at the door as the other boys did; why one day I would propose marriage and the next announce I was entering the monastery; why my moods changed faster than Al Maguire could get thrown out of a basketball game. If they could see and understand that, then I would be able to laugh about the time we staged a food strike.

As is probably true for many people, there are at least two of me in history. There is the Brian who wore the costume and the one who ripped it off. There is the Brian who made noises to distract attention and the one who now wants to talk about being gay. There is the Brian who met others' expectations and the Brian who struggles with his own. I don't understand why I had to go through those painful experiences, but I don't hate the other Brian any more than the butterfly hates the caterpillar.

Today, however, instead of investing my energies attempting to reconcile the differences for those "who knew me when," I prefer to spend my time working to make sure those gay people who follow this generation need not be as alienated by their youth.

THE MARCH

December 1979

Since moving to Boston, I have walked Jeremy, my Irish setter, around the same path each day, and from time to time have spotted a handsome young guy clipping lawns and hedges. Sometimes he would smile at me with interest, but generally he would make eye contact and then look away shyly. He's gay, I decided. He's probably fifteen, gay and doesn't know how to deal with it. I wrestled with what approach I should take. Remembering how isolated and frightened I felt in high school, I wondered whether I should introduce myself and subtly reveal my sexual orientation. Then he would have someone with whom he could share his secret. Yet, would I be introducing myself if he wasn't attractive? Maybe I shouldn't start something. Besides, what if he's straight? What if he's a homophobe? I have to live in this neighborhood. Better keep walking.

Finally, after three and a half years, we spoke our first words. "What's the dog's name?" he asked, looking up from his weeding. "Jeremy," I responded, feeling an embarrassed rush. "Nice dog." "Thanks." "See you later." "Yeah, see you later." After a few more of these brilliant exchanges, we learned each other's names. "His name is Caleb," I told Ray. "He's a senior in college—older than we thought—but I still think he's gay." Perhaps next spring I'll ask him. Yard work is finished for the year.

"Brian," I heard an excited voice shout as I was marching with about 100,000 other gay men and lesbians down the streets of Washington, D.C. "Brian," I heard over the laughing and cheering and singing and chanting and clapping. "I *knew* you were a homosexual!" screamed the familiar figure who made his way through the crowd. "Caleb!" I exclaimed. "I knew you were gay too." Then from behind me came a chorus of "Hi, Caleb!" from the large contingent carrying the banner of one of Boston's most popular bars. So much for the "isolated and frightened" theory.

A bit later in the day, as I was looking out from the speaker's platform upon the jubilant sea of gay humanity which stretched in powerful waves to the base of the Washington Monument, I spotted a ruggedly handsome, mustached man waving and smiling at me from the front ripple of spectators. I waved and smiled back. Another brother intoxicated by the spirit of the moment, I thought. At the end of the presentation, however, the young man was awaiting me behind the platform, his hand still waving, his smile still glowing. As my body swelled with that all too familiar sensation of guilty excitement, I strained my eyes to see more clearly. "FRANK," I gasped. "I can't believe it." It was my younger brother's best friend from high school, whom I hadn't seen in ten years. We kissed and hugged and exchanged quick stories between our cheers for the bold declarations of independence which were resounding from the stage. "If you're ever in New York . . ." he insisted as he walked backwards into the mass. "I promise . . ."

Caleb and Frank are only two of the many familiar faces spotted in the parade and rally which brought together a mighty army of lovers from throughout North America. They are only two of the many thousands of stories which are being told and retold to friends back home who ask marchers, "What was it like?"

It was like nothing I had ever been a part of before. It was magic. It was spiritual. It was energizing. Though clouds threatened us throughout the day, I remember it as bright and nippy. The sky was aglow with multicolored flags, placards and banners which proclaimed the good news of being gay—of being gay and from San Francisco; of being gay and from Atlanta; of being gay and from New Mexico, Alaska, Oklahoma, Michigan and Missouri; of being gay and religious; gay and atheist; gay and black, white, red, yellow, brown; gay and young; gay and old; gay and proud; gay and alive, gay and whole. "We are everywhere," we chanted as we marched to the beat of kazoos and tambourines. "We are everywhere," we screamed as we danced and skated and skipped like children. We embraced each other with shiny-faced grins of excitement. We renewed each other with winks and squeezes and out-stretched arms. "We are everywhere," we insisted, "and we will be free."

Funny thing. I didn't want to go to the march. I was upset by the reports I was getting about the planning process and the division it was causing among community leaders. I felt black-mailed into going. I thought that I had to be there for the mere sake of body count. I wish that my friends across the country who didn't go had been there. They too would have been de-lighted. They too would have been healed by the day of unity we experienced. That's not to say there weren't things we can't improve upon next time. And there will be a next time.

Next time I want to be one of 500,000. Next time I want to walk through the crowd and see the faces of my high school basketball coach, the lifeguard at the pool and my fraternity pledgemaster. I want to be able to throw my arms around the Brother who taught me English senior year, and to kiss the guy who after school used to watch "Adventures in Paradise" with me. Hell, I want to kiss Gardner McKay! I want to see more nuns and more GIs and more grandparents. Next time I want to see a bishop hold up his half of the sign which reads, "We are Everywhere."

Incidentally, the minister who lives down the street has a son who might be there. I think he's sixteen and feeling isolated.

MY FAMILY

July 1980

A few eyes swelled with tears at a recent Gay Pride march when the crowd passed a young woman and her father holding the sign: ALL AMERICAN LESBIAN AND HER DAD FOR GAY RIGHTS. More than one smiling person nudged a friend with a "Look at that!"

I don't imagine Dad and I will ever be holding up such a sign. It's not his style. But he isn't beyond calling Anita Bryant a "horse's ass" nor saying he feels my participation in the movement is "important." Mom wouldn't hold a sign either, but she does end all her letters to me with "Our love to Ray." There is special affection for my lover in my family. My younger brother even introduces him as his brother-in-law.

The support goes beyond the immediate family too. At cousin Patty's fancy garden wedding, she insisted the photographer take a picture of all the cousins and "cousins-in-law." The large group gathered, took assigned positions and readied themselves with a big "cheese." "Wait a minute," insisted the bride, "where's Ray?" He was in the bathroom. "We have to wait for Ray," she and the others declared. The photographer waited, the cousins waited and a number of very befuddled guests whispered, "Who's Ray?"

In a recent Gallup poll, 80 percent of those interviewed said the family is the most important part of their life or one of the most important parts. Gay men and women comprise at least a representative number of that group. In fact, for many gay people, reconciliation with family is an important step toward self-acceptance.

Without my family, I would be less whole. Without their love and support, I would be less happy being gay. Like other gay people from close families, I find strength in my past and draw courage from knowing there is a small army of McNaught relatives around the country who love me as an openly gay person.

It hasn't always been so ideal. Six years ago, when I came out publicly, there was enormous tension between me and my immediate family and little communication with other relatives. Dad made it clear that if I were to appear on a certain television program, I was never to return home. Mom called my apartment several times and just cried. Sisters and brothers vanished.

My self-affirmation as a homosexual caused them great confusion and embarrassment. Though dialogue was strained, gradually each family member let me know how my "new" life was affecting theirs. The folks quit going to church. My older brother got into a fight with his boss, who made a crack. Even my youngest sister protested that all the publicity would discourage boys from asking her out. "My life is ruined," she is quoted as saying. They were all hurt and they felt betrayed.

How do you get from such a point of alienation and hostility to a space where the folks are now asking for extra copies of my articles to send to their friends, and my younger sister calls from college because she needs a good quote for her term paper on homosexuality? Was it just a matter of time? No, but it does require time for all healing to take place. Was it because they loved me so much? Love is surely essential but just love is not enough. Actually, the transition required a variety of factors.

Primarily, we gay people who come out to family and who wish to maintain intimate ties need to love ourselves, do our homework, be patient and trust the love of our families. We can't expect parents to be supportive of us as gay people if we communicate we are not happy being gay. If we don't love ourselves as homosexuals, how can we hope others will? Likewise, we can't expect Mom, Dad and the kids to know anything positive about homosexuality. Like most of the world, they only have negative stereotypes with which to work. When we come out, they're going to have questions and we need to be able to answer them. That is why we must do our homework. Being gay doesn't make you an authority on homosexuality.

Mom wanted to know whether I was going to hell and I had to be able to answer her in a language she could understand and trust. If I couldn't answer her, I needed to know a source which could. My older sister wanted to know whether she caused my being gay. "Remember the time. . . ," she would say and proceed to recall an event from our past. With her, too, I had to alleviate guilt by providing accurate information. You don't have to be a theologian or psychiatrist to answer these basic questions. You merely need to do some basic reading.

Your parents need to do some reading also. I gave my folks Laura Hobson's *Consenting Adult*, a novel about a family coming to grips with a gay son. They trusted Hobson's objectivity and found her story very helpful. Also highly recommended are: *Loving Someone Gay* by Don Clark, *Now That You Know—What Every Parent Should Know About Homosexuality* by Betty Fairchild and *A Family Matter: A Parent's Guide to Homosexuality* by Charles Silverstein.

Patience is the next step. It takes time for people to learn new information and to change their expectations. Patience for me meant answering the same questions from time to time; not confronting the family with displays of affection they couldn't yet handle, understanding that silence doesn't necessarily mean anything other than "I'm confused."

If there was love there to begin with, if the family celebrated a certain special closeness, it will endure. With time, my family learned I was still the same Brian. I still loved to sing. I still cracked jokes. I still figured a way to get out of doing the dishes. If anything, my coming out enhanced my relationship with my family.

Some people feel we shouldn't waste our energy on our families, especially if they haven't responded affirmatively to our being gay. I suspect that many of those people have never found family to be an important part of their lives. Mine, however, is a treasure and worth every nurturing effort. Even though the folks might not march, there have been times when gay friends have watched me interact with my family, poked each other with a smile and said "Look at that!"

A TRIP TO
THE GYM

June 1984

My friend John and I just signed up for a year's membership at the local gym. At thirty-six years old, I have never had the body I wanted or, I suspect, anyone else did either. John is forty-five and wants to flatten his stomach. We both decided it was again time to invest in our self-image.

From what we hear, our small-town gym attracts many Mr. America types. We wouldn't know this for sure because we make it a point to show up at 9:00 A.M. when the place is empty. In that way, no one will see at what level I set the Nautilus weights.

There is something very serious and something very comical about my trips to the gym. I find a lot of humor in reflecting on the first week of workouts. Being the type of person, for instance, who would vacuum his house before the cleaning service arrived, I did my share of emergency sit-ups and push-ups at home before I felt ready to walk into the gym for the first time.

As a result of recently quitting smoking, I was terribly constipated and, subsequently, loaded with gas during our initial visits. Seeing how the first three or four machines stretch your legs up and apart, I kept giving John and the instructor plenty of breathing room. "You all go ahead," I encouraged, "I want to pace myself."

Other humor was found on the floor as we attempted to lift our legs over our heads in a backward somersault.

"Come on, guys, lift those legs higher," commanded the handsome, friendly, well-built, no-wedding-ring-on-the-finger instructor.

"Oh, Bob," I offered, "this is John's *very* favorite one."

The humor seems to make it easier for me to walk into that environment. For most of our lives, the thought of entering into a gymnasium and into the sacristy of straight male machismo—the locker room—has struck terror into the hearts of many gay men. I found, during my first week at the gym, that if I laughed a lot, I didn't have to admit how intimidated I felt by what was expected of me or how frightened I was of failing. Focusing on the comical aspect also distracted me from the painfully serious side of this issue: my sadness and anger that I have spent so much of my life fighting the fear that I am not fully a man.

It makes me sad and angry that at so many moments in my life I have been afraid of being discovered as a fraud; afraid of being a major disappointment to my father and mother, my older brother and older sister, my younger brother and younger sister, my grandfather and grandmother, my childhood friends who picked me to be on their team, my gym instructor, my girl friends, my fraternity brothers, my readers and now, by God, even to other gay men!

As I go to select the Nautilus weight I will lift, it makes me sad and angry to think about how many hundreds of upset stomachs I have had fearing that I would strike out at bat, drop the fly ball, cry in front of other boys when I hurt myself, get into a fistfight, cross my legs or look at my fingernails in an "unmanly" manner. In other words, the fear of failing each new test.

As I slip into my gym clothes now, it makes me sad and angry to think of how many times and how many ways I have kept my body covered because I didn't think it measured up to what I should look like—my arms were too skinny, my muscles too small, my chest too flat. It is a sad thought to know that you have hated your body. Yet, because of that sense of inadequacy,

I loved winter and bulky sweaters; I would decline invitations to go to the beach or the country club; I would shower before or after the other campers, dorm residents or monks.

Perhaps the saddest and angriest I have ever felt about this constant struggle was when I realized that gay men can intimidate me as badly as straight men do. The one and only time I went to the baths many years ago, I nervously walked around the maze in my towel for an hour or so. It took an awful lot of energy to build up the nerve to go to the baths in the first place, as I believed the ads which suggest that everyone there is a hunk. I was relieved to discover that this ordinary body of mine was in the company of other equally ordinary bodies, but then I happened past two men who were sitting together reading the local gay newspaper. One of them, who was reading my syndicated column, looked at the picture, looked at me, poked his friend and said something. What I imagined hearing was "He doesn't have a body!" I was crushed, embarrassed and upset. Had they just said what I most feared would be articulated by someone, somewhere? I sought the fastest route possible back to the locker room and the safety of my clothes.

To my surprise, I have found in my travels that many gay men feel similarly sad, similarly angry and similarly intimidated. When I get the opportunity to do workshops with gay men at colleges or conferences, I focus a lot of our time together on body image. It is an exciting, threatening and liberating time for almost all of the participants, the majority of whom have never talked candidly with another gay man on how they feel about their bodies.

"It's a hot summer day," I will say, "and we've just arrived at the beach in the company of other gay men. I want all of you who would strip off your shirt immediately to go sit in the right-hand corner at the front of the room. I want those of you who would wait to take off your shirt until you spotted people in less good shape than you to go sit in the left-hand corner at the back of the room. In the center of the room, I want those of you who would keep your shirt on all day."

Group number two is always the largest, with group number one and group number three generally drawing equal numbers. And, regardless of the age group, the observations made and the conclusions drawn by the men are very much the same. The men observe how relieved they are to know that other gay men feel the same way about their bodies and they express shock that many in the room don't feel better than they do. They recall, with some humor, the various times they have sat in the sun with their shirts on or declined invitations to go home with someone for fear of exposing their love handles. They also talk about the number of drinks it takes them to relax in the bar, so that by the time they let go of their feelings of inadequacy, they're drunk. They talk about how they live for the nod of acceptance from someone better looking and of how that which attracts them most also intimidates them most.

They conclude that gay and nongay media create images of male youthfulness and virility which, though sexually stimulating, nonetheless create unreasonable expectations of what is normal. They conclude, with enthusiastic certainty, that our body image, our feelings of adequacy, are all too often dictated by how others feel about our bodies rather than how we feel about our weight, height, skin and hair color, measurements, complexion and so on. The goal, we decide together, is to focus on how we each feel about our bodies, to be realistic about our expectations and to learn to work with and love what we have.

It is a worthy goal. My problem is that I don't know what I have to work with. I have never reached my limits because I have always feared the process, the initiation into virility, the test of endurance, the risk of failure. For years I have focused my and other's attention on my face and my mind. But now I want to know what my potential and limits are. I want to go to my grave feeling that at one point in my life, at least, I really liked my body, I conquered my fear of failure, I was the first to take my shirt off at the beach.

RECLAIMING
THE HOLIDAYS

December 1984

The holidays can be a tough time of the year for nearly everyone, particularly for gay men and lesbians. The rituals surrounding Thanksgiving and Christmas, especially, place such traditional emphasis on family that many gay men and women experience painful loneliness and alienation. Yet, I feel, it is not the holidays which cause the turmoil but rather our expectations of them.

Every carol sung, every Salvation Army bell rung and every television special aired can remind us of the magic of our youth, when love seemed unconditional. The jarring contrast with today's reality of estrangement from family because of our sexual orientation can make every carol a dirge and every bell an annoyance. Instead of embracing the holidays as an opportunity for creating new adult gay magic, some of us stand like young orphans in the snow, peering through the frosted window with hungry looks for the security of the past.

To ensure that we get into the Christmas spirit, many of us will sit silently, out of arm's reach from our lovers, and cry our silent tears of joy in front of the television, night after night, as estranged Scrooge is embraced by his nephew and niece in *A*

Christmas Carol; as estranged Ed Asner embraces his estranged draft-dodging son in *The Gathering;* as estranged Jimmy Stewart is showered with affection by his family and friends in *It's a Wonderful Life.* "That's what Christmas is all about," we whisper to our souls. "Christmas is people being good to each other; embracing each other as friends." And our souls whisper back, "You mean it's our family embracing us as we are; because we are."

With such expectations, Christmas can cause terror in many of our hearts. For some of us, the terror is in knowing that we must go to our parents' homes; for others, the terror is in knowing that we can't go to our parents' homes.

Those men and women who have not come out to their families often spend the holidays playing charades. Without words, they repeatedly seek to act out to Mom and Dad the message: "Quotation. Four words. 'I am not straight.'" Their expectation is that if their parents gently guess that they are gay, they will be families just as close as Ed Asner's by the end of the movie. They don't come right out and say "I'm gay" because that's against the rules and such a hostile act might mean that they wouldn't be welcome in their families homes at Christmas.

It's important to these gay men and lesbians to be home for Christmas, just as it is for most Americans. Among our expectations for the holiday are that we will be in a warm and wonderful family home and that, if we live in New England, it will snow on Christmas Eve.

Once again, the expectations get in the way. Often it doesn't snow on Christmas Eve, even in New England, and often the family home of the closeted gay man or lesbian at Christmas is not warm and wonderful. These gay men and women rarely relax. They see how their married brothers and sisters with children are treated more like adults than they are. They endlessly dodge baited questions about romantic endeavors from family friends they never liked. They wonder to themselves how many relatives would pull them under the mistletoe "if they only knew." This isn't the way it is supposed to be, they think.

Many of these closeted gay men and lesbians have lovers with whom they live the other fifty-one weeks of the year. They put up trees, just like their folks did, and they bought each other special gifts, just like their married brothers and sisters did, but their trees are not lit in their homes for Christmas and their gifts were opened a week early. These two "roommates," unlike their folks and unlike their married brothers and sisters, will seek Christmas magic separated from each other. "I love and miss you. Merry Christmas," they whisper to each other on telephones behind closed doors.

Those gay men and lesbians who do come out to their families can be broken down into three categories during the holidays: Those who are not welcome home under any condition; those who are welcome home under certain conditions and those who are always welcome.

Openly gay men and women who are not welcome in their parents' homes during the holidays have two choices. They can either mourn or they can change their expectations of their families and of the holiday and make it a fun, magical, meaningful time.

Lesbians and gay men who are welcome in their parents' homes under certain conditions probably make up the largest group. While one will find goodwill in many of these homes, you aren't likely to discover much peace. Everyone is a little tense. Although Mom and Dad are happy because no one is missing from the dinner table and the gay son or daughter is happy because there is still a place set for them at the table, the dinner table is more of a conference table and everyone is a little tense that the terms of the treaty will be violated.

The spoken or unspoken conditions imposed by some parents or even by the lesbian daughter or gay son often include the request that the subject of homosexuality not be raised in front of young children or persons outside the family; that if "what's-his/her-name" really must come, the two of them refrain from any public displays of affection and that proper attire (particularly in the case of women) be taken home for church and Christmas dinner. Despite what they wear, with this atmosphere of peaceful coexistence, the Christmas dinner is quite unlike that celebrated by the Waltons. Though everyone is assembled at the same table, no one tastes the food. You just eat, smile and search for safe subjects.

Christmas and the other holidays of the season ought not to

Martinak, Wendy

be like that, I think. Christmas and Hanukkah, Thanksgiving and New Year's Day ought to be festive, happy periods when everyone has a gay old time. If the holidays aren't pleasant experiences for us, if our expectations of them are not met, then perhaps we have only ourselves to blame.

Christmas does not belong to heterosexual married couples with children any more than the flag belongs to a single political party or the Bible belongs to a single religious group. One need not spend Christmas in the home of one's parents in order to experience the magic of the holiday any more than one needs snow, turkey, a fireplace or Bing Crosby's voice on the radio.

There needn't be dramatic changes of heart on Christmas Eve, like that of Scrooge, in order for you to be "light as a feather" on Christmas Day. Your parents don't have to love you; Santa Claus doesn't have to visit you; Ed Asner doesn't need to move you to tears in order for this holiday or any holiday to have meaning to you as a gay man or lesbian.

The only essential ingredient for a successful holiday is that you love yourself. The only valid expectation for the holiday is that you have the right to determine what you want it to mean to you and how you will make it meaningful.

Check out your expectations. It's okay to recall with a smile the Christmas magic of your youth, when love seemed unconditional, as long as you remind yourself that you continue to be unconditionally lovable. Then listen for the Salvation Army bell, watch the television specials and sing those Christmas carols, particularly "Deck the Halls." It drives some straight people crazy when they have to belt out "Don we now our gay apparel."

PROUD GROWLS
AND
COURAGEOUS ROARS

September 1984

The Cowardly Lion traveled to Oz because he was ashamed of being a "sissy" and wanted the Wizard to give him courage. To survive in his jungle, he needed the "noive" to put a bite in his growl.

Many of us, it seems to me, make a daily trek to the Wizard in search of the necessary mental and moral strength to persevere. We, however, find to our delight that you can be courageous and a sissy too.

I would guess that on an average day, the majority of gay men and lesbians are called upon to be courageous about their sexual orientation at least five times. Those of us in relationships, for instance, decide whether or not to kiss our lovers in public when we part for work and when we return home. We all are asked, "Who answered the phone when I called?" or "What are you reading?" (Better yet, what are we *not* reading in public?)

How do we respond to the credit card, hospital, insurance and telephone survey questionnaires: "Married or Single?" To the antigay television show, newspaper column, headline and joke, the Wizard within us says "Call the station. Write the newspaper. Don't laugh!" How do we respond?

Very few people are able to or should be expected to respond courageously to every opportunity and every challenge, but I believe that the majority of gay men and lesbians rise to the occasion with a proud growl at least once a day. The gay freshman might not speak up in class during a morning discussion on homosexuality, but may walk across campus in the evening to the gay and lesbian support group meeting. That's a growl.

The lesbian librarian might kiss her lover behind closed doors in their suburban home at 8:00 A.M., but at 1:00 P.M. may be ordering extra copies of a new book on homosexuality. That's a growl.

The gay police officer may not challenge a "fag" joke at roll call, but later in the day might drive around the gay bar to make sure the patrons aren't being hassled. That's a growl.

Those women and men who growl with pride at least once a day by boycotting Coors beer, by buying a lesbian album or gay novel, by not laughing at a remark about the late Truman Capote's affectations or by coming out to yet another person are the army of sissy lionesses and lions who unknowingly guarantee the changing of society's attitudes and laws. It needn't be a dramatic gesture to have a dramatic effect. Often unbeknownst to them, each time these proud growlers make a statement about the truth and beauty of their lives by acting or reacting courageously, they change reality, either their's or someone else's. Sometimes no one is around to see that they turned the channel when Jerry Falwell appeared or to see that they sent a donation to Rep. Gerry Studd's reelection campaign, but *they* know they growled and they feel freer, more whole and more integrated.

Once or twice in a lifetime, the growl becomes a courageous roar which sends reverberations through the entire jungle. The roar is a mighty proclamation of self which is so powerful that it often startles even the sissy lioness or lion who made the noise. They didn't know they had it in them and they certainly didn't plan it. Nevertheless, when the moment came, when the challenge was thrown their way or the opportunity was presented to them, they responded with great strength and provided us all with a true profile in courage.

The history of the modern gay and lesbian civil rights movement is the history of proud growls and courageous roars. It is a history of people who have learned to make the necessary noises to protect their sanity and to guarantee their safety. The daily growls are what keep us all going. The courageous roars, which now fill all corners of the jungle, give us models of authentic living.

A middle-aged religious Brother, working with the poor in the South, recently provided us with such a model. His letter to me stated, "My reason for writing is to let you know of a recent event in my life. It was completely unplanned but rather significant for me."

The Brother, whom I met many years ago at a Dignity convention but hadn't heard from since, was among 600 members of his religious order attending a special conference. The gathering was designed as a time for the men to examine their own and the order's commitment to the Gospel. Among the speakers, provided for inspiration, was the venerable Archbishop Helder Camara, internationally respected head of the Recife, Brazil, diocese and an outspoken champion of the poor and oppressed. The humble teaching Brother was one of three men chosen to publicly respond to the message of the archbishop.

In the midst of his talk, Archbishop Camara referred to homosexuality as "a very special problem. This distorted sexual use is a physical or spiritual illness; a manifestation, many times, of insecurity; a consequence, at other times, of drugs."

The nervous Brother listened intently as the two other respondents ignored the comments on homosexuality and focused, instead, on different aspects of the archbishop's address. "I was reluctant to challenge such a genuinely good and heroic figure," the Brother wrote to me, "but for the benefit of the 600 Brothers, I did."

"Some of us have lived through change and confusion and have had enough of it," he said to a hushed audience, the smiling archbishop looking on. "Others of us feel we, no matter how old, can—and must—be converted. So I ask you, Dom Helder, can we be converted to a new church, a new world view, a new awareness of the oppression? Are we part of that oppression? Are you, God forbid, also part of that oppression?

"You ask for audacity and so I presume to offer just that. In every gathering there is a sizable and vulnerable minority that is fair game for condemnation and hurt. If it is true, as the most common statistic seems to indicate, that one out of every ten persons is homosexual, a good number of any group you address fits that category. To say that homosexual persons suffer from a physical or psychological illness or that they are insecure perpetuates a set of myths. Just as people who have persecuted you have sometimes felt they were doing a service to God, so also there are those who feel the same about homosexual persons.

"Therefore, just as you have learned to love the poor by being with them, perhaps all of us can learn the nobility and goodness of those who find they are, through no choice of their own, indeed homosexual, by associating with them. As you have invited us to do, there ought to be a change from a monologue to a sincere dialogue with gay people."

That was a roar.

The Brother's courageous response to a challenge was unplanned. "I felt good that without much planning I had actually made the point with our Brothers that gay people cannot be dismissed with worn-out myths," he wrote. "Not too many years (months?) ago, I would have chosen to ignore any possible confrontation. I do not like to become controversial. Why I actually took up the point, when the two previous reactors overlooked it, I cannot say, but I'm not sorry. In fact, I'm rather proud of myself."

The road to Oz and the courageous roar of self-affirmation can be a lifelong trek but it won't necessarily be. Traveling sissy lions and lionesses should take pride in their daily growls and realize two things: The growls of pride make it significantly easier for others around us to walk safely. Secondly, there's no telling when the Wizard within will turn up the volume on a growl so that what the world hears is a roar and the subsequent words, "I'm rather proud of my self."

I LIKE IT

November 1978

The young medical student finally blurted out the question which had been gnawing at him. "Do you ever regret being gay?"

"No," I said with a growing smile. "Sometimes I regret being so totally identified with my sexual orientation, but I never regret being gay."

"Wouldn't you really rather be straight?" asked one Jewish talk show host. "Would you rather be Christian?" I asked.

"Think of all the hostility you face," commented one black woman. "Because of that, wouldn't you prefer being heterosexual?"

"Who's telling whom about hostility?" I queried. "How much would it take you before you wished you were white?"

As supportive as they might become, many straight people have a lot of difficulty thinking of homosexuality as an intrinsic part of a person's psychological makeup. Even if they can be convinced that gay people didn't choose to be gay, they still need to hear us admit we would rather be like them.

I like being gay. I like knowing there is something very unique and even mysterious about me which separates me from most of the rest of the world. I like knowing that I share a special secret with a select group of men and women who lived before me and with those special few who will follow.

I like walking at life's edge as a pioneer; as an individual who must learn for himself the meaning of relationship, love of equals, sexuality and morality. Without the blessing of the Church and society, my life is one outrageous experiment after another. I like knowing that if I settle into a particular frame of thought, it is because I have found it appropriate and not because I was raised to believe that's the way things must be.

I like knowing that I can go anywhere in the world and meet someone who will smile that knowing smile which instantly says "Yes, I know; me too. Isn't it nice not to be alone? Hang in there." It is a twinkle and a smile which results not from being white or male or Catholic or American. It is a secret smile which only gay men and lesbians exchange.

I like exchanging that knowing smile with waiters in Galveston, flight attendants in Terra Haute, theater ushers in Detroit, salespeople in Boston and sunbathers in Sarasota. I like to give and receive those smiles at Mass, at lectures, in department stores, at the laundromat and on the street. I like the feeling I'm not alone.

I like believing the studies which indicate gay folk are generally smarter, more creative and more sensitive than nongay folk. It makes me feel chosen. I like knowing that a gay man's dinner party will usually be more elegant, that a gay-orchestrated religious service will usually be more artistic and that a gay disco will generally be more fun.

I like knowing that there is far less class division to be found at most gay parties. Janitors and lawyers and truck drivers and librarians are bound to unknowingly bump elbows and even likely to sit next to Lily Tomlin, Paul Lynde or half of the Ice Follies.

I get a kick out of knowing that antigay people are probably wearing clothes designed by a gay person, living in a home decorated by a gay person, attending a play performed by a gay person and participating in a Sunday service celebrated by a gay person.

I laugh when I think of antigay men cheering gays on the football field and learning about other scores from a gay sportscaster. I especially love the thought of antigay Catholics praying to gay saints.

I like being gay for all of these and many more reasons. Primarily, though, I like being gay because it is an essential aspect of who I am . . . and I like myself.

◆

UNDERSTANDING
SEXISM

1982

Most women I know are sexist. Most homosexuals I know are heterosexist. Most blacks I know are racist. Most Jews I know are anti-Semitic. It is the rare soul who has deprogrammed herself or himself today.

When you meet a woman who doesn't consider herself a person without a penis; who rejects a preconceived role; who celebrates the gifts of her womanhood and who sees equal rights not merely as a justice issue but as an opportunity for society to become enriched, spend some time talking with her. Consider what such a woman has overcome.

Can we men imagine growing up in a world in which every supreme authority is female? What if God, Jesus, Santa Claus and the breadwinner in our family was a woman? What if every U.S. president, every judge, every visible police officer, every priest and rabbi, every major author and corporation president was a woman? What would that do to our sense of importance, our sense of pride, our sense of equality?

What if men's penises were thought of as elephantiasis of the clitoris? What if male body hair was socially offensive and we were forced to daily shave our underarms, legs and chest?

What if we had to resort to electrolysis or bleach to remove that which grew naturally? What if male puberty was considered a "curse," wet dreams disgusting and semen a frightening sight which should be disposed of with a sanitary napkin? What if our culture demanded that men insert devices into our penises to prevent pregnancies? What if developing massive pectorals at age fourteen was viewed by society as essential if we wished to get a date?

Speaking of dates, what if we weren't allowed out at night unless a girl asked us out? What if women stood every time we went to the "powder room," opened every door, pulled back every chair and paid every check? Would we not feel weak and dependent as opposed to special?

What if we only had two sexual role models in life, the whore or the saint? What if girls who peeked into our locker rooms when we were naked were considered red-blooded and when we did the same to them, we were labeled "sluts"?

What if a limited family income only allowed our sister to go to college because boys don't need an education to be happy—they merely need to meet a successful woman? Besides, our only career options would be teaching and secretarial work.

What if we finally did get a job in the women's world and discovered that to compete we had not only to be equal to women but better? And what if we found that on payday, women were paid nearly twice as much for the same job? What if a successful male was always described as being cute or handsome rather than sharp, intelligent and industrious?

Would we not be angry? Would we not become assertive—even aggressive? We would not begin demanding that womankind share power with us? Would we not demand that language be changed to reflect the presence of men in the world, and history books be changed to reflect the achievements of men in history and customs be changed to reflect the self-sufficiency of men? Some of us would but many of us would not.

Given those circumstances, many of us men would be afraid to challenge thousands of years of culture. Many of us would fear that if we boldly proclaimed our disgust of the status quo, women might not date us, like us or stay friends with us. We would fear the reaction of our families and male friends. Worst of all, many if not most men would have a hard time

believing that we were equal to women. While we talked about pride, we would feel in our gut that there was really something basically inadequate about being a man. We would ask women to help us understand ourselves just as we had in the past when we plopped ourselves down on the couches in the offices of women psychiatrists, the examining tables of women doctors and the pews of women spiritual leaders. We would be sexist because we would believe that if we had our druthers, we would really rather be women. To paraphrase the line in *Animal Farm*, "All people are equal but women are more equal than men."

As a man living in a male world, I acknowledge my sexism. I work hard at eliminating it, but it shows its ugly face more often than I would like to admit. I have attempted to understand what it is like being a woman, but it is difficult to feel fully the rage most women do or should feel. My best bridge in spanning the emotional gap between myself and women is my reflections on what it is like growing up homosexual in a heterosexual world. As a homosexual who is outraged by my heterosexist tendencies, I feel more comfortable suggesting the awful truth that many women today are sexist.

Heterosexism and sexism are prejudices based upon the assumption that one sexual orientation or one gender is more equal, more preferred, more "normal" than another. Most of our battles against heterosexism, sexism, racism, anti-Semitism and so on have been based upon arguments of injustice. But even when arguments are cogent and we are successful in eliminating inequalities, we don't succeed in eliminating prejudice; we don't root out of ourselves and others the sexism, for instance, which is at the core of the injustice. What has helped me attack my own heterosexism is the process of examining not only why my sexual orientation is just as good as that of heterosexuals but, more importantly, what makes me special. I am less likely to be heterosexist when I begin celebrating the unique beauty of my being gay and the unique contributions I am making to society and nature because of my homosexuality.

My sexism and that of my women friends is best attacked when I examine, with the tutoring of women, the unique beauty of the female, the unique glory of the female perspective, the unique contribution to society and nature of the female

mystique. I don't owe it to women to eliminate my sexism by discovering the unique perspectives and gifts of women; I owe it to myself.

As most men today, I have been deprived of half of reality. It's as if one of my eyes and one of my ears have been eliminated; as if I have only been allowed to eat predesignated foods and read preselected books; to smell only half of the flowers; to encounter only half of the truths. Men have deprived me of my entire inheritance as a human being by burying half of life's treasure under mounds of ignorant, self-serving bias. I am less whole because of this deception. I am less healthy, less liberated, less in tune with nature because of this deception.

If we doubt there is a special new beauty to be discovered, it is our sexism, our years of indoctrination which gives birth to and nurtures those doubts. To challenge those doubts and to set about the task of discovering the whole melody of creation is an exciting, compelling adventure. It is for that reason that I suggest that if you meet a woman who celebrates her womanhood, do yourself a favor and listen to her song.

MAKING ALLIES
OF
MARRIED GAYS

November 1985

Not long ago, a brief handwritten note arrived at the house which angrily begged for a response.

"After 22 years of marriage, my husband tossed your book into my lap and walked out the door. You're the expert. What am I supposed to do now?"

I am certainly no expert and I had no quick and easy answers. What I did have was lots of old biases about married homosexuals which I tried hard not to let get in the way. I wrote back to this woman, who undoubtedly blamed me and my book on being gay for the dissolution of her dreams, and attempted to address the issues which I believed she was facing, such as a sense of betrayal, feelings of failure and the dread of hopelessness, among others. More importantly, I recommended a couple of readings, including Don Clark's *Living Gay*, and I gave her the names of two women friends in different parts of the country who also had been married to gay men and who agreed to talk with her.

At the time, I lamented that there were no support groups, of which I was aware, for spouses of gay men and lesbians. I feel that talking, crying and laughing with people who are also strug-

gling with your issues is the best way to formulate and answer your own questions. Now, to my great pleasure, I find that there are a number of such groups available across the country. Every minister, counselor, therapist or friend of heterosexually married gay men and women and their spouses take note.

It is very important that we openly gay men and women who are not in heterosexual marriages direct our attention to those who are, particularly at this time. In the past, for a variety of regrettable reasons, married homosexuals have not always found much reliable support in the gay and lesbian community, particularly if they wanted to continue being married.

The reason it is especially important that we who are openly gay now invest some of our energies in people who are in the closet of a straight marriage goes beyond the simple issue of compassion. An enormous percentage of the men who frequent public rest rooms, baths and the bushes are married. Because they often don't read gay periodicals, nor are they always willing to be honest with their physicians, many of them are horribly ignorant of safer sex practices. As such, many experts believe that bisexual and gay men who are married to heterosexuals will be the conduit for the spread of AIDS to the next high-risk group, their unsuspecting wives and their future children.

Another reason for working hard to help married homosexuals and their spouses come to grips with homosexuality is more selfish in nature. We need their help. As AIDS hysteria continues to sweep the country, our homosexual kin, who have attained social acceptance by their marriages, could prove to be responsible voices at parent-teacher meetings, parish council sessions, at public hearings and in letters to the editor. If married homosexuals are enabled to come out to themselves and to their spouses, both will then have the potential to be our strong allies rather than our foes, which is too often the role many have played.

According to a survey I conducted for the city of Boston, 12 percent of the gay and lesbian respondents had been heterosexually married. I have heard estimates as high as 20 percent for those who are now openly gay and were once in straight marriages. If, however, we were able to poll all of the estimated twenty-two million homosexuals in this country, I suspect that we would find the vast majority of them are currently in heterosexual marriages. In other words, because of the incredible pres-

sure to marry in this culture, openly gay men and lesbians are only the tip of the homosexual iceberg.

In a section on "Married Gay Men" in the book *The Joy of Gay Sex*, authors Edmund White and Dr. Charles Silverstein suggest four reasons why homosexual men marry women. Some gay men, they say, marry to "cure" themselves. These individuals, sometimes with the encouragement of misguided ministers and therapists, believe that a wife and family will rid them of same-sex fantasies. The second reason for marrying is to provide yourself a cover. These men, according to the authors, know that they are gay when they marry and they have no intention of curtailing their same-sex activities. They do, however, want all of the privileges which society bestows upon married people.

Some homosexual men marry to please their families and their straight therapists. To that list, I would add those who marry to please God. Finally, a fourth reason for marrying is love. The authors state that some gay men truly love the women they marry and wish to spend their entire lives with them. They may do so with the hope that their spouse's love will incorporate or accept their homosexuality.

Most gay men who marry women probably do so for a variety of reasons, including today, the fear of AIDS. Surely there are men who feel that it is too risky for them to develop a relationship with a person who may have been exposed to AIDS. Again, there is the false hope that a heterosexual marriage will somehow enable them to alter or control their true sexual feelings.

Gay men undoubtedly *stay* in straight marriages today for a variety of reasons too. Some gay men stay married because they truly love their wives and they don't want to end the very special friendship which they have developed with them. If they have children, there is even more of a reason to sacrifice personal satisfaction for what is perceived to be the greater good. Some gay men stay married because of AIDS or because they are afraid they won't be able to compete in the gay "marketplace." Other gay men have such a distorted image of what it means to be gay that they are unwilling to accept that label for themselves. They have strong biases about openly gay people.

Many openly gay people also have strong biases about married homosexuals and those who claim to be bisexual. Nearly every gay man and lesbian has paid a high price for his or her

honesty, sometimes with the loss of a job or the loss of family. Seventy-six percent of the people who responded to the Boston survey said they had been verbally abused for being gay and 24 percent had been physically attacked. Against that price tag, gay men and lesbians sometimes see married homosexuals as having some of the privileges at none of the cost.

Further exacerbating the rift is the experience openly gay men and lesbians have had with some closeted married homosexuals in the pulpit and in the state house. The unwritten code of honor, which prohibits yanking unwilling people out of the closet, forces gay people to sit silently by as closeted ministers rail against them and as closeted legislators vote against them.

Bisexuals are eyed with great suspicion as individuals who are too cowardly to accept a gay label. In both the heterosexual and homosexual communities, they are viewed as wishy-washy. Like all of these biases, this is unfair and inaccurate.

Married homosexuals and their spouses, if they have made that long and incredibly difficult journey out of lies, expectations and propriety, often stand alone in the middle of a battlefield with the two warring factions telling them what to do. Guns from both sides are pointed in their direction and their love, integrity and sense of self-determination seem doomed to be maimed in the cross fire.

We must, I feel, support the journey of every gay man or lesbian in a heterosexual marriage and we must hope that the decisions they make about coming out to their spouse and about staying in or leaving their marriage best suits their needs and not ours. The support groups which have been established across the country for gay and bisexual men and women in heterosexual marriages and for their spouses are designed to help people help themselves to make the best decisions possible under the circumstances.

To obtain a list of all such groups, in order to pass it on to a friend or to a health care agency, minister or counselor, send a stamped, self-addressed business envelope to Charles Piersol, Box 10041, Rochester, NY 14610. A retired social worker, therapist and organizer of a support group for married gay men, Mr. Piersol has compiled an important listing of twenty-two groups for married homosexuals and bisexuals and eight groups for their spouses. He is also very interested in hearing from any person who belongs to a group which should be listed among the others.

Because of his efforts, the next time some departing gay spouse tosses my book into someone's lap, this "expert" will have a better response to the question, "What am I supposed to do now?"

SICK OF HEARING
ABOUT AIDS

October 1984

Most people I know are sick of hearing about AIDS. It wasn't long ago that many people complained that AIDS was being ignored as an issue and now these same people are sick of thinking about it and sick of worrying about it. Some people even just turned the page because they're sick of reading about it and they doubt that I could make AIDS interesting, inspiring or funny.

I'm sick of AIDS too, and I'm sick of the reaction I get when I talk about it. I brought the subject up in front of my parents and they became uncomfortably quiet. I brought it up at a dinner party and people started complimenting the soup. I brought it up at a public lecture and my opponents smirked.

Talking about AIDS is generally boring and depressing. It is also overwhelming. I can't keep the medical jargon straight; I have no idea how much research money is enough; I'm defensive with straight people and I have visions of being quarantined. I would just as soon not talk about or think about AIDS ever again, but my friends don't give me much choice.

My buddy, Bill, is one who wants to talk about AIDS. His last letter spoke of nothing else.

"It's not pretty, AIDS isn't," Bill began. "Even my basic body odors are new and unfamiliar.

"There is not a part of my body from the waist up which doesn't hurt. My hands are still recovering from where old I.V.s blew them up like footballs. My chest contains a constant heartburn and I'm weak and skinny at 130 pounds. Below the waist—I've been told to forget there is anything there. . . . Once my lungs cleared up enough to get me off the respirator, they moved me out of intensive care and I picked up an intestinal bacteria which generally is fatal with AIDS people—having the bowels simply run until there's nothing left. I beat that and then the little purple KS tumors came out, followed shortly by genital herpes on my butt. . . ."

When a person you love is fighting for his or her life against AIDS, it's not likely you will be smug about AIDS. Bill, Michael, John, Dennis and Dave are five friends who are currently struggling with or have died because of AIDS. Thousands of people to date have contracted AIDS, some of whom may be your friends too. They do not want *us* to be bored by the subject.

AIDS may be boring and depressing to think about, but ignoring it won't make it go away. It could be years before researchers have a vaccine for AIDS, and even longer before there is a cure, if ever they discover one. My special friend Bill will probably be dead by then. And by then, probably every gay man and every lesbian, every parent of a gay person and every friend will be dramatically affected by AIDS. Each one of us may well be numbed by news that a friend has died because of AIDS. We may also be shocked to realize how many of our civil liberties have been nibbled away and how much political ground has been lost. AIDS will not eliminate the gay community, but it clearly has the potential to politically, emotionally and physically maim this and the next generation. The extent of its effects can be somewhat determined by us.

We can't allow ourselves to get smug about AIDS. The number of friends we lose might be determined by how informed we become and how willing we are to change the atmosphere at a dinner party by talking about AIDS. The amount of

liberty and political ground we lose can be determined by how many of us stay out of the closet rather than retreat behind closed doors; by how many of us fight together against the finger pointing of our enemies and how many of us maintain our self-esteem.

Larry is another friend who doesn't give me the choice as to whether I will think about AIDS. He coordinates the efforts of local volunteers who administer to the needs of people with AIDS and who work to educate the community and the public.

"It's amazing to me that people think AIDS is going away," Larry said when I read him my letter from Bill. "A lot of people still don't even know the symptoms of AIDS or how to avoid it. I was doing some AIDS education work at the baths and this very handsome thirty-year-old man wanted to know if he was high risk. He told me that he has been going to the baths eight times a month for the last six years and that he does *everything*. I said, 'Sit down!'"

A peace activist in the late sixties and early seventies, Larry suggests that AIDS is the Vietnam of the gay community. "It's unpopular; it's divisive and the casualties will be about the same," he said. He then talked with alarm about the number of gay people he sees going back into the closet because of AIDS; the number of lesbians and "good gays" who are pointing fingers at gay men with AIDS and the number of gay men who are walking away from friends who have AIDS. "It's very frustrating," he said.

On behalf of my frustrated, though hopeful, friends Bill and Larry, I offer ten simple, easy-to-remember guidelines to thinking about AIDS. They help me make AIDS less boring, less confusing and less frustrating.

1. AIDS is transmitted by semen. Until further notice, don't swallow semen and don't engage in anal or oral sex without a condom. I have lots of fun with the other options and you can too.

2. If you love your gay male friends, repeat this first guideline to them as often as you can. Your friends in relationships need to hear this as much as those who are single.

3. If a friend has AIDS, hold his or her hand, write him funny notes and tell him that although you don't know what to say, you love him.

4. God played the same role in spreading AIDS in the gay community as God played in the destruction of the Dade County orange crop.

5. AIDS has nothing to do with *being* a homosexual and it's nothing about which to be ashamed. It's risky behavior, not risk groups, which spreads AIDS. Running to the closet makes you no healthier, prouder or safer. It can, in fact, have the opposite effect.

6. Go to an AIDS fundraiser, write a check to a volunteer group or offer some of your time once in a while.

7. Vote for people who are publicly committed to funding ongoing research into a vaccine and cure for AIDS. I trust the National Gay and Lesbian Task Force to tell us when enough money has been allocated.

8. As Sr. Digna would say, "When you point a finger at someone, three fingers are pointing back at you." There are not "good gays" and "bad gays." There are good and bad health practices.

9. Nothing lasts forever. AIDS, too, will pass, but not for some time.

10. AIDS is too serious to ignore. We must be concerned, do what we can to prevent it and meet the needs of those who have it. And then we must all smile, celebrate life and be gay. One of the important lessons we have learned from AIDS is how to live life to the fullest.

MEETING
NEW PEOPLE

September 1980

The most pressing question for the gay people I meet is not how to survive in a hostile world but how to meet other gay people. How do you make friends and how do you find a lover?

We have been systematically isolated from each other for fear of what acknowledging our homosexual feelings would mean to us socially. When we finally do dare to acknowledge our nature and go looking for mutual support, we generally enter a subculture of bars which continue to isolate us. God bless the bars for being a place to gather, but I know people who have frequented the same watering holes for ten years and have yet to establish a significant friendship. They have slept with plenty of people but have never had a stimulating conversation with another gay person. The tragedy of this is most glaring when someone from the bar community is murdered and the morning paper quotes unidentified bar patrons as saying, "I saw him frequently but I don't know anything about him."

Part of the problem is with the environment of many of the bars. The loud music and dim lights discourage conversation. Part of the problem is with society and the penalties it enforces for being gay. Many gay bar patrons still fear public exposure if

they tell too much about themselves to the person on the next stool. However, most of the problem, I feel, falls on the shoulders of the individual and his or her expectations of what will be found in the bar.

While there are some exceptions, the majority of people I know who frequent gay bars are in an endless search for Mr. or Ms. Right. And if they aren't searching for the perfect person, they're generally in pursuit of the perfect orgasm. What we all probably know in our hearts but fail to acknowledge is that there is no perfect person awaiting our arrival and that no orgasm has much significance outside of a relationship. Each person is flawed in some way but has the potential to be a wonderful friend and lover. Sexual experiences outside of a relationship are like a whiff of poppers or a toke of grass. They frequently provide momentary pleasure but generally are only a distraction from the real need to love and be loved.

Relationships of love and support with other gay people, I think, are essential to our happiness. (Lovers are basically friends with whom we choose to share our lives in a more intimate way.) But all relationships begin with risk. We risk that we will be rejected. We risk that we will have our investment of time and energy wasted. We risk being hurt. But we also risk being loved, accepted, supported and embraced, and that makes the risk worthwhile.

When do you take that risk? Significant relationships are made possible when the two people share some common ground. Too often in the bar scene that common ground is simply that both people are gay and both find the other physically attractive. Experience suggests that's not enough upon which to build a friendship. Much of our desire to bed down an attractive person is based on our own feelings of inadequacy. If we can get that "hunk" to take an interest in us, we reason, we must be okay. Even in these situations, many potential friendships end after the first sexual encounter because one or the other is less than totally satisfied with the sex they shared. They didn't talk to each other, so they don't know what common ground they share. Further, they fail to acknowledge that few people experience great sex the first time with another person. Sex is like a pair of new shoes. It is frequently only with time that it becomes comfortable and fully satisfying.

I don't think good looks or a nice body belong at the top of a person's checklist of desirable traits in a future friend or lover. (It's nice to be in a relationship with a handsome person, but it's funny how good-looking the person you love becomes with time.) In fact, appearance might be number twenty-one in this list of twenty things my friend Sol Gordon looks for in a friend.

"People I like," writes the well-known sex educator, "have a sense of humor; have a passionate interest in something; have high energy levels; are tolerant of my changing moods; know how to listen; are creative; enjoy touching; are enthusiastic; exude self-confidence; appreciate my successes and are sympathetic when I fail; appreciate when we can be together and don't fuss when we are not; have a sense of justice and injustice; are sensitive to the needs of others; can take risks; have an air of mystery about them; are not sure of everything; are optimistic; don't make fun of people; can offer love unselfishly; are people in whose presence I like myself more."

Your list may vary but the point is that we all have things we look for in other people. When deciding whether or not to risk ourselves in a potential relationship, we need to know whether we share significant common ground with the other person. What is even more important is our own determination to be the kind of friend and lover to others we hope to have them be to us.

But how do you meet these people? In every city which has an identifiable gay community, there are political, religious and social organizations. (If you are unaware of these, they are listed in the local gay newspaper or can be found by getting a copy of *Gayellow Pages* from Renaissance House, Box 292, Village Station, New York, NY 10014. Tell them where you live and they will send you the complete guide to gay-oriented organizations, bars, periodicals, etc., in your section of the country.)

The people who join these organizations are looking for the same sort of support system we all seek. While you may not be enthusiastic about their political stance, religious views or their social activities, you are not committing yourself to them by attending one meeting. You are merely putting yourself in a setting where you may have your first meaningful conversation with another gay person.

While conversation in the bars is more difficult, it is not

impossible. Before opening your mouth, it's important to remember that everyone who surrounds you is equally shy, equally nervous and equally hungry to make friends. The tough exterior of some is their way of pretending they are mean and macho. That's supposed to be sexy. If you don't talk to them, they, like yourself, will undoubtedly go home frustrated, lonely and feeling a little stupid about the charade.

Pick out the people in the room who look as if they are being most themselves. Walk over, smile, stick out your hand, say, "Hi. I'm just looking to make friends tonight. My name is . . ." If your gesture is rejected, the other person will probably kick himself or herself in the morning. At least you tried. The alternative to trying is living a frenzied life among people who will say, "I saw him frequently but I don't know anything about him."

◆

HOW TO
FIND A LOVER

February 1986

Even before AIDS was an issue, one of the most commonly asked questions in the gay and lesbian community was "How do I find a lover?" Today, the question takes on a new urgency as many gay men are convinced that a lover will not only ensure that they are happier but also healthier.

I don't feel that everyone needs a lover to be happy, or healthy, for that matter. Safer sex practices seem to guarantee that a person's need for intimacy can be satisfied, as it was before AIDS, for the rest of the individual's long healthy life. The fear of contracting AIDS seems to be a foolish reason for entering a relationship and a poor excuse for staying in one.

But what about those gay men who say, regardless of AIDS, that they want to be in a relationship? I don't feel it is unfair to suggest that the majority of openly gay men over thirty who *really* want to be in a relationship probably already have lovers. There are a lot of gay men over thirty who insist that they really want lovers but how many of them really, *really* do?

Not everyone is a relationship-oriented person, despite what they think. I happen to be. In a couple of months, my

partner Ray and I will celebrate ten wonderful years together. Each of us is nourished by our relationship; our mutual love and commitment indeed makes us happier and healthier people. Should something tragic happen to either of us, the other would grieve terribly at the loss, but we both know that sooner or later the survivor would enter another relationship. We are at our best when we are in a relationship.

Unfortunately, most everyone thinks that they ought to be or need to be in a relationship in order to be happy. Heterosexuals, particularly women, have similar misconceptions about having children. Yet, just as not every heterosexual woman is happiest with a family or necessarily makes a good mother, neither does every gay man need a relationship to be happy or make a good lover. I feel that gay men who are not relationship-oriented can be far happier and healthier if they admit to themselves that they prefer living alone; that they like doing things their own way, at their own pace; that they are at their best when they have many friends but are uncommitted to any single one.

Gay men who are not relationship-oriented and who have not accepted that fact, spend many, many years feeling frustrated because they are alone. They are unaware that they unconsciously tend to make it impossible for themselves to be in a relationship. They unconsciously sabotage the various opportunities for relationship which present themselves on a regular basis. They are generally unaware of the elaborate mental checklist they have created which prevents them from finding anyone acceptable with whom to have a relationship. Such a gay man experiences a lot of peace when he admits to himself that he likes living alone.

But what of the gay man who is relationship-oriented? How does he find a lover? When such a man asks me the question, I offer a few observations before I offer him a map. For instance, I suggest that it is far easier for an openly gay man to find a lover than it is for a gay man in the closet. That may seem obvious, but it isn't to everyone.

Being in the closet limits your options. Being in the closet often means that you are afraid to subscribe to a newspaper or magazine created for gay men. It can mean that you are afraid to attend a Mass, a lecture or a social gathering tailored for gay

men. Being in the closet generally means that you unconsciously send out the message "I don't like myself. I don't like being gay." Unless it is another self-hating homosexual you seek to attract, not liking yourself is not an attractive feature. For these and many more reasons, a person who really wants to find a lover really has to take steps out of the closet.

If the person asking for help finding a lover is under thirty years of age, I encourage him to enjoy his teens or twenties. Psychologists generally suggest that we will feel more ready to make commitments in our early thirties. Youth is a time for experimentation. That may mean entering a relationship, as I did and from which I learned many things, but I feel the time is better spent dating, finding out more about yourself and the world in which you live, securing your education, exploring the work world, developing a mature relationship with your parents. In other words, if you have soured on being in a relationship because the one you entered in your twenties didn't work, try again and trust that you are now better equipped to make sacrifices and the commitment to love and be loved.

The most successful relationships are those in which two adults, mutually attracted to one another, come together for the benefit of both. It is wonderful if there is magic in the beginning of a relationship, but there needn't be. It is terrific if there is "hot sex" in the beginning, but there needn't be. What there needs to be is communication, honesty, sacrifice, a willingness to compromise, respect of the other's integrity and individuality, a good sense of humor and commitment. Love is less those tingly feelings which begin the relationship than it is the beautiful fruit of many years of hard work. Any gay man or lesbian who is in a relationship or who hopes to be is urged to read the excellent book, *The Male Couple—How Relationships Develop*, by David McWhirter and Drew Mattison.

Now, how about the map? One more word of caution. Don't go looking for a lover because you won't find one. Go looking for a friend and if you really want a relationship, that friend can become a lover. Like many gay and lesbian couples we know, Ray and I began as friends.

Begin your search for friends by deciding in advance that you are going to be an active participant rather than a passive observer. You aren't going to meet many interesting people by

standing silently in the corner of a bar for hours waiting for someone to ask you to dance or sitting quietly by the telephone for weeks waiting to be asked to a party. Just as good safer sex requires that you talk about what feels good, making friends requires that you speak up, initiate conversation, introduce yourself. Being shy is no excuse. We're all shy.

Be aware of your approach to life. Is it traditionally male (predatory) or female (relational)? My approach to love, to people and to life is heavily female. It is far more important to me that the person with whom I sleep be a nice person. If he has a great body and a nice face, I'm pleased. A more traditionally male approach would be to bed down with someone because he has a great body and a nice face and to be pleased if he is also a nice person. If I ask you to dance, it is because I want to dance with you. Someone else may ask you to dance because he wants to go to bed with you. Be aware not only of how you approach life, love and dancing but also that not everyone approaches things the same way.

You can meet friends anywhere—in bars, gyms, through classified ads, church, political organizations, restaurants, dances, college classrooms, at work and in the laundromat. Obviously, if the space caters to gay people, you have a better chance of meeting a gay friend there than you would in a space which is open to the public. Once again, the more open you are about being gay and the better you feel about it, the greater the chances are that you will feel free to pursue and attract gay friends throughout the day and not just at night.

Finally, I feel that one of the best means of meeting gay friends is by having people over for dinner. Encourage old friends to bring a guest. If you are invited out, say yes with the hope of making new connections. Keep building that circle of friends, because even if you don't find a future lover through this means, you will certainly make new friends. By knowing ourselves and knowing our needs; by coming out and speaking up; by getting out and surrounding ourselves with other self-affirmed people, we're all guaranteed to be happier and healthier.

◆
DEFINING
COMMUNITY

October 1983

"There's no such thing as a gay and lesbian community," some people argue. "There are only men and women who share a sexual orientation and oppression."

It is true that our community is different from the black, Hispanic and Jewish communities. The frustration expressed by those who feel no sense of community reflects their expectations that we should have the same sense of bonding that they imagine blacks, Hispanics and Jews have.

If all homosexuals came from families in which every member was homosexual, then it would be fair to compare ourselves to the ethnic and racial communities. But gay men and lesbians are orphans and our community is a collection of orphans. We have no patriarchy or matriarchy to provide us established leadership as do those communities of people whose oppression is a family affair. We are like strangers who have been dropped on an island together. Because we have no tradition, no relevant laws, no history of organized struggle, we have no basis for determining who will lead us and what our priorities will be.

To further complicate our attempt at building a community, our rejection by family—our orphaned status—prompts us to demand that we be each other's loving and supportive sister and brother, mother and father, doting aunt and accepting

FRIENDS AND
LOVERS

1982

Like their heterosexual peers, most gay men and lesbian women seek to share their lives with friends and with lovers in relationships of mutual respect and support. Having been isolated from each other from the very beginning, having been denied the important growth process of dating and courtship with a person of their own choosing, having to live in a world which promises to punish them for affirming their homosexuality, many gay people, particularly those who have just recently come out, can find it difficult to meet new friends, to build a healthy love relationship and to make it last. Family, church and society generally are unsupportive and unreceptive. Fortunately, it is much easier to meet other gay people today than ever before. One of the great advances of the gay and lesbian movement has been the establishment of an identifiable community. It is a strong, diversified community, found easily in any major city, in which individuals can experience understanding, acceptance, respect and support. And it is in this community that one can make some very special friends. With hard work, a good sense of humor and the willingness to compromise, these very special friends can become very special lovers in relationships which offer us all models of determination, loyalty, caring and celebration.

ace. We expect that we will all agree upon our needs and work collectively, generously and without criticism toward meeting those needs. We too often expect that any person who is gay or lesbian will support the cause by eating at our restaurants, buying our newspapers, donating money to our campaigns, patronizing our bookstores, marching in our parades and, at the very least, voting in the elections we deem critical. When we note that a full 10 percent of the general population is not eating, buying, donating, patronizing, marching and voting "the gay way," we become frustrated and bitter.

I have felt that frustration and bitterness. On many occasions in the past, I have thrown up my hands with disgust, feeling that I had been wasting my time on a group of selfish, lazy, ignorant, heartless, spoiled people, many of whom took for granted the changes in gay and lesbian life in which they hadn't raised a finger to assist. I, too, have lamented "There is no gay and lesbian community." But I expected too much. I wanted a gay and lesbian Walton's Mountain and I felt I got a gay and lesbian Tower of Babel.

Today, I celebrate our diversity and applaud our accomplishments. In fourteen short years, we have created a strong, viable community which offers safety, support and hope, and we have created strong, viable communities which offer the freedom of individual expression in a familylike atmosphere. If a person is gay or lesbian, he or she can come out and be supported by a youth group, a college group, a parents group and a group for older gay men and women. You can be into leather, feathers, Church, witchcraft, music, law, politics, anarchy, health, muscles or chubby people, and we have a group for you. There are gay and lesbian neighborhoods, restaurants, bars, newspapers, recording studios, bookstores and churches. If you like to march in the streets, the community provides that option. If you hate gay politics, there are plenty of tribes who would welcome you. Our strength is in our diversity.

When I first came out, I expected that every gay man and lesbian would love me and that I would love anyone who said they were gay. When I realized that not everyone thought I was the neatest thing since sliced bread and that not everyone I met who was gay was someone I would want to hug, I changed my expectations and I began to build my own community.

Is there a gay and lesbian community? It is what you make of it.

FRIENDS AND
LOVERS

MAKING IT LAST

February 1977

It was Winnie the Pooh—his adorable pudgy arms out-stretched in a futile attempt to capture a delicately beautiful butterfly. "Oh Pooh, how I do love you!" the inscription read. "To John, with love, from Brian, Valentine's Day, 1971."

It was my finest offering, representing hours of drawing and precise blending of pastel watercolors. When it was finished, it was ceremoniously placed on a dining room table—an "altar" surrounded by flickering candles, an uncorked bottle of burgundy and two goblets. There it and I waited anxiously for John's arrival from work.

But like Pooh's efforts to capture the butterfly, the wait was in vain. John didn't come home from work. He preferred, instead, to be with someone else. It was Valentine's Day—the celebration of erotic love, and I sat frustratedly alone.

It was this dashing of expectations which led me into my first gay bar, where I ceremoniously bought drinks for the house. "Happy Valentine's Day from Brian."

In retrospect, the memory is overflowing with humor. My bar bill was moderate, given the fact that it was only 8:30 P.M. (How was I to know that no one really arrives until a fashion-able 11:00 P.M.?) But at the time, it was a nightmare of an eve-ning. I plied myself with gin and tonics, screaming inside for relief from disappointment. As a hopeless romantic, struggling to believe that gay love was no different than straight, Valentine's Day represented every hope for a happy, fulfilled future. I watched that hope being regurgitated into a wastepaper basket next to the living room couch where I deigned to suffer my fate and greeted the morning with a resolution to end my life and all the pain which accompanied it.

Eight years have passed—eight years, three relationships, a hundred probings with couples and individuals seeking counseling and a thousand conversations with gays from Bangor, Maine, to San Diego, California. After all of that time, all of that listening and speaking, all of that reading, digesting and regurgitating, all of that love gained and love lost, I far more understand Pooh and his futile effort to capture the "elusive butterfly of love."

Valentine's Day, the commercialized celebration of hearts, flowers and "love means not having to say you're sorry," should have far more significance for gay men and women than our annual celebration of the Stonewall Revolt and the birth of gay liberation, for it is our inability to come to grips with love which cripples us as a people more than our inability to proclaim on national television that we are avowed homosexuals.

The pursuit of love is the most basic common denominator to all persons, be they male or female, gay, straight or bisexual, black, white, yellow, brown or red, 1-year-old or 140. Love is an absolute which defies difference. The sooner we gay men and women accept that, the sooner we will liberate ourselves to experience its richness.

As a person who has been invited to speak to and hear from assemblies of gay and straight individuals across the country, I have encountered the position on love from radical feminist separatist to Roman Catholic cardinal. I have heard defenses of open relationships, monogamous relationships, auto-relationships, group relationships and no relationships. Modeling my earthly wondering and wandering on a Siddhartha-like trek, I have abandoned all preconceived notions, experimented with new ideas, espoused an openness to all expression and maintained a policy of nonjudgment.

I have heard, believed and enunciated that gay people are different from straight: Gay expression of love, because it is outside cultural expectation, is more honest and liberating; we are pioneers in the area of relationship and our greatest offering to civilization is the beauty of sexual freedom.

Bunk!

Likewise, I have heard that gay men and women are promiscuous; unstable; unable to satisfy a sexual hunger.

Again, bunk!

While it is true that the isolation gay persons are forced into during the "Wonder Years" prompts a certain behavior and while it is true that the lack of societal encouragements such as tax benefits, religious ceremonies and peer pressure can make stable relationships more difficult to maintain, gay men and women ultimately seek the same stability and fidelity, the same richness of love that nongay persons seek.

Maintaining a firm commitment to refrain from offering to anyone absolute criteria of judgment, I nevertheless offer here a hypothesis which has proved personally enriching.

Experience, observation and the voice within insist upon a belief in pure love being approached as an absolute which permeates the existence of all things living and dead (dead is not the proper word but is used to describe those things—plants, animals and persons—whose earthly forms have deteriorated). That love is called God, soul, life and a variety of other terms. Our ultimate goal as persons inside and outside the human form is to experience the perfection of love. Just as experiencing the perfectly developed body requires hard work and pain, so too does experiencing perfect love.

Love, though One entity, is multifaceted and is expressed in a variety of stages. There is the love that a mother has for her child, which is based upon a dependency. There is brotherly love (or sisterly love), which culturally has never called for sexual expression. And there is erotic love—the love of Valentine's Day, the love of sexual partners, the love which brings people together into relationship.

A primary stage of erotic love is physical attraction—nice placement of chest hair, nice breasts, nice face, nice . . . and so on. That progresses into being attracted to the person's mind, the person's sensitivity to people—the deeper, more aesthetic values of personhood.

In erotic love, we attempt to break down the barriers which separate us from the objects of our love. We seek to get to know people better—to have them know all there is to know about us and to learn their uttermost secrets. For us, that is a sign of intimacy—of union. Most of the world we see around us does not go beyond this stage of development. Most see this candid sharing as being the essence of love—its ultimate manifestation.

Once the last morsel of secrecy has been revealed, there is a letting down of enthusiasm. The magic is gone, as some people describe it. The honeymoon is over. Boredom sets in. The body, which once caused an immediate excitement, has become as familiar as the old painting on the wall which no longer elicits wonder. The personality, which has been completely revealed, shows signs of frailty and failure, inadequacy and shortcoming.

"Why should I spend the rest of my life with this number," we ask, "when there are so many exciting people out there with whom I could be really happy?" We long for the exciting days of discovery again—the days of finally disrobing the body we were only able to fantasize about before. We long for the flowers, the little gift surprises, the intimate dinners over candlelight, the newness of background, family and so on.

And so we break up. We divorce. We move out and on to better horizons. We fear stagnation in our early years and leap back into the race before it is too late to compete.

"The consequence," writes Erich Fromm in his acclaimed *The Art of Loving*, "is one seeks love with a new person, with a new stranger. Again the stranger is transformed into an 'intimate' person, again the experience of falling in love is exhilarating and intense, and again it slowly becomes less and less intense, and ends in the wish for a new conquest, a new love—always with the illusion that the new love will be different from the earlier one. These illusions are greatly helped by the deceptive . . . sexual desire."

The most obvious question is "Why bother?" Why should I spend the rest of my life with someone who no longer excites me physically (especially when I have a very strong sexual drive and there are so many gorgeous specimens waiting to be discovered); no longer excites me intellectually; no longer fascinates my probing mind nor satisfies my emotional needs?

In fact, argue some, why should I stay with a person who is causing me emotional pain—a person who is being cruel and unloving? I have no desire, they state, to spend the rest of my life with someone I am going to be constantly fighting.

In order to go beyond this critical stage—this period when excitement has waned and boredom set in—there would have to be a mutual understanding of what possibilities might lie ahead. What is the carrot which leads us on?

Where are the examples? Most persons can't point to their parents as representations of the fine gifts involved in love's higher levels. Many heterosexual partners who have "stuck it out" did so because of "the children," religious and cultural pressure and the fear of what they would do if they actually did break away. With the softening of sanctions against divorce, more and more persons are declaring their freedom and singing the praises of such a move.

If, historically, those couples had shared the dream and goal of love's ultimate gifts, then I would have to accept their experiences as proof positive that this illusive carrot is a lie. But it hasn't been tested properly and has only been written about in abstract terms. Even the Church, in its naivete and lack of understanding of Christ's real gift, has insisted upon fidelity under pain of serious sin. In this, it has failed.

"To love somebody," states Fromm, "is not just a strong feeling—it is a decision, it is a judgment, it is a promise. If love were only a feeling, there would be no basis for the promise to love each other forever."

Why make such a promise? Because, after love has left the stage of the selfish and emerged into the level of the selfless, the human spirit begins to experience a perception, a unity and an internal peace which is otherwise totally impossible. That perception, that unity and that peace defy description by persons who have not experienced them. All of us, at one time or another, have touched for the briefest instant the perfection of spirit. Abraham Maslow calls those moments our "peak experiences."

Commitment to one individual, while not excluding love for all other individuals, enables us to come face to face, soul to soul, with the dynamic power which unifies all of life. "Erotic love," states Fromm, "if it is love, has one premise. That I love from the essence of my being—and experience the other person in the essence of his or her being. In essence, all human beings are identical. We are all part of One; we are One."

By eliminating the traditional reasons for loving another and going beyond their lovability, we enter into a cosmic sharing of life-love-God-essence-what have you.

A Zen Buddhist psychotherapist described it to me as a mountain jutting into levels veiled from the city below by a fog. The overwhelming majority of people live at the base of the mountain, totally oblivious to the possibilities of climbing. From the city, you can see small fires built on the sides of the mountain, indicating the places where others have dared to climb. The largest gathering of fires is shortly above the city. Like a pyramid of light, they decrease in number as the mountain increases in height. The climb up the mountain represents the levels of selflessness. The ultimate experience of letting go brings the individual to an awareness which cannot even be imagined from the valley below.

Jesus spoke in terms of giving sight to the blind. The Pharisees, who had the faculty of sight, were blind, according to Jesus' narrative. His life, which merited Him the designation of divinity, was the ultimate expression of selfless love. As such, He was totally comfortable with all persons and stands out as the historic example of ultimate peace. I have come, He said, so that the blind may see.

We constantly remind ourselves that *gay* is an adjective and not a noun. The gay person who seeks to experience ultimate love; who seeks to build his or her fire at the top of the mountain; who seeks to see has the same opportunity as any other person.

My experiences in relationships prompt me to admit that I could not make such a journey with everyone. One lover, with whom I spent a couple of years, presented obstacles over which I don't think we could have come, especially at that stage of my development. My second lover would have been a beautiful traveling companion had we known enough to share the same vision, thereby enabling us to overcome the boredom period which everyone encounters.

There are several real-life everyday obstacles which gay men and women, in particular, have to face. For instance, most gay people have been locked up for so long that we are like puppies who insist on sniffing every bush in the park. While our heterosexual peers were initiated into the rituals of dating throughout high school and college, we either pantomimed or refused to cooperate, thereby being denied the very essential period of psychosocial development. Coming out threw us into a candy shop where we could finally touch and feel the bodily warmth of that which before we could only fantasize. We are in a fetal stage of sexual development. Hopefully, history will be sensitive to that when describing our emergence. With the same hope, perhaps all persons who grow up in this country in the near future will be able to experience the ritual of dating and courtship at the same age, despite sexual orientation. (I would love to be a chaperone at a high school senior prom where gay students danced together with as much excitement and comfort as their straight classmates.)

In addition, even if an individual is raised in an open and healthy environment, psychologists and sociologists do not expect persons to make definite choices about anything until their early thirties. Dr. Daniel Levinson, professor of psychology at Yale University, states emphatically that persons between the ages of twenty-two and twenty-eight naturally avoid strong commitments, preferring to "hang loose." It is not until an individual passes through the early thirties crisis that he or she begins to make long-lasting commitments to job or relationship.

If that is true for nongay persons, how much more likely and natural it is for gay men and women to refuse to limit their options. Dr. Levinson would argue too that the age at which a gay person felt comfortable making long-lasting decisions would inevitably come later in the thirties, given the obstacles to their developing adulthood.

(A side effect of this analysis is the light it sheds upon the difficulty often encountered in relationships between persons separated by many years in age. One is naturally prepared to settle down while the other, just as naturally, is not.)

Another element which must be considered in gay relationships is children. "Unless human beings are close to children they have little ability to think about the future," insisted Margaret Mead, internationally renowned anthropologist. Gay people, she stated, should involve themselves in households which are microcosms of all of human life . . . older people, children, women and so on.

How often have we seen or witnessed the emptiness which surrounds a family holiday, such as Thanksgiving or Christmas, when celebrated by individuals without a family. Even the coziest gay couples often find themselves longing for the squeals of a youngster and the teary reminiscences of an oldster.

The extended family offers gay couples the opportunity to

satisfy the natural desire to give direction and nourishment to the young and relieves the fear of growing old and disabled alone.

I have, of course, avoided the head-on question of the role sexual freedom has in the personal commitment to one individual. Does emotional fidelity necessitate sexual fidelity? If love of a particular one prompts a universal love of others, what does that say about our sexual expression of that love?

Reserving the proverbial option to change my position, I believe that sex and love have been foolishly linked as being one and the same. I also believe that we are foolishly preoccupied with the subject of sex. It possesses us and drives us. It has the power to totally control our lives, making it impossible to think clearly.

Persons who have lived long periods of time together testify that sex gets better and better, lending credence to the belief that sex is most wonderful when it is a total expression of selfless love. We have also heard persons argue that their sex has been enriched when they have had the freedom to express themselves outside the home or when they and their beloved are engaged in a threesome. The question of sex and the role it plays in a person's development and attainment of selflessness is an open issue from my present level of consciousness, but I am comfortable in affirming one guideline: If you are ready to make a permanent commitment to another person, and that person in his or her current stage of development is not able to cope with nonmonogamy, don't throw it all away in the name of sexual license. That's like opting for a lifelong wheelchair because your driver's license has been suspended. The opposite is also true. If your lover's commitment to sexual freedom is preventing you from committing yourself to making the journey together, relax. The sexual appetite will mature.

While it is entirely possible for everyone to live out his or her human existence jumping from one magical moment to another, never having to face the calling to grow beyond immediate satisfaction of artificial needs, life here and beyond here offers experiences in personal wholeness, unity and peace which are within our reach. To choose the opposite is to take Pooh's fixed place on the page, a constant distance from ever reaching the elusive butterfly.

MONOGAMY

Why is it that many gay men have as much trouble mentioning the word *monogamy* with their friends as a closeted homosexual would have with the word *gay* at a Knights of Columbus convention? If you say it over and over again in front of a mirror, it doesn't sound dirty at all.

Once upon a time, I thought monogamy was the only framework a relationship could have in order to be *legitimate*. That attitude undoubtedly reflected my Irish Catholic background and my paranoia that a lover would leave me if I gave him the chance. But from my reading of popular gay literature and from traveling to a variety of gay conferences, I learned that I was unsophisticated; worse yet, I was unliberated. Before that time, I thought that I would be perfectly happy settling down with someone for the rest of my life, but by talking with some liberated gays I learned that true gay happiness results when you can romp in the hay with anyone you want, whenever you want. Not wanting to be unliberated, I went home and proceeded to destroy in my foolishness what was a wonderful relationship. Having secured my freedom, I entered the Garden of Bliss and eagerly approached the Trees of Pleasure. I ate to my heart's content, expecting that I would never again hunger. However, after a period of time, I noticed that I was wasting away to the point that I hardly recognized myself.

Soon I encountered another pilgrim who had also followed the siren song into the garden. He, too, looked a bit emaciated. After a while, we decided that we liked each other very much, but it was difficult to see each other clearly because the fragrant and lush leaves of the trees blocked out the light and came between us. So, deciding that we were both hungry for something we couldn't find in the Garden, we took each other's hand and walked out together. Risking the label of "unliberated," we built our own garden.

In agreeing upon monogamy as a fence for our garden, neither of us is suggesting that we don't frequently long to run naked through the Garden of Bliss. Our nocturnal emissions and auto-erotic behavior are often centered around the sights we encountered or imagined we would encounter there. Nor does it mean that we will pick up and leave if one of us breaks down the fence on a lonely day and quickly ducks into the lush foliage. It means merely that we have a shared vision of the kind of garden we would like to build together, and experience has taught us that bringing in plants from the other garden will eventually guarantee that ours will be overpowered. We have no desire to break up the plants.

Having an ideal relationship is not unlike having an ideal of the physique you would like to develop or the level of spiritual wholeness you would like to experience. If someone asks you "What will it be like?" you will be unable to answer until you develop it. For the time being, all you have is an idea of what you believe will make your life the best possible experience.

As discipline is required in building a body and establishing an intense level of spiritual awareness, so too is it called for in creating a love relationship. If you wish to develop your body into a beautiful specimen of human form, you begin restricting your diet and your time. You cut back on foods which will contribute to fatty love handles; you turn down invitations to go to the movie on Tuesday night because that's your night to work out at the gym. You strain yourself deliberately because you know that building muscles isn't easy. If it was, everyone would be a Colt model. To develop a strong spiritual base, as is the intention of the Trappist monks, you discipline yourself by going to bed early and rising early. Your day is routinely divided into scheduled sessions of individual and communal prayer. You

OPEN
RELATIONSHIPS

March 1977

When David brings home a trick, John moves into the guest room. The next morning, John looks forward to meeting and talking with the stranger who occupied his bed for the night.

David has one night out of the week set aside by mutual consent during which it is expected he will go out and not return until morning. Sometimes he will bring home a friend with whom both he and John can relate physically.

Peter and Mark have been living together in San Diego for eleven years. Though they haven't had sex together in ages, they are lovers. Genital gratification is sought outside the home.

In both cases, the two persons who have come together in a relationship have no doubts they will spend the rest of their lives together. They love each other to the point that they are willing to make a commitment to be a part of each other's joys and sufferings.

Neither couple is presented here as an *ideal* way of maintaining a relationship. But they do help to illustrate a point.

Human intelligence and our sophisticated means of communication have liberated us to establish our own dreams, our know that Thomas Merton did not write *Seven Story Mountain* after staying up until 11:30 each night to watch "Flash Gordon" reruns.

Likewise with a relationship. While you don't have the ability to verbalize the exact form or the levels of selfless love you will experience, you know from past practice what contributes to mutual growth and what destroys it. As with everything else, you make sacrifices which aren't easy to make. After three relationships and an extended period of liberation in the Garden, my observation is that monogamy is the best road I can follow to achieve what I believe will be an incomparable experience.

Monogamy, in this sense, cannot be used as the answer to jealousy and possessiveness. Those are the natural feelings which accompany infatuation, not love. Nor is monogamy the best route for everyone. Not everyone wants to have a beautiful body, given the price, nor does everyone seek to achieve great levels of spiritual awareness, given the sacrifices. Perhaps monogamy isn't even necessary to make work what Ray and I hope to achieve in our relationship, but neither of us was able to make it work when we were liberated and neither of us wishes to sacrifice this relationship in the effort.

own course and our own method of actualizing both in our lives.

Throughout the world and throughout time, individuals have entered into relationships with other individuals for a variety of reasons. We read with astonishment about marriages that were arranged by parents before the children were born. We hear about persons in their eighties and nineties joining in wedlock. We know that the marriages of kings and queens were most often political alliances. While rampaging through the bar, looking for a pretty face, with thoughts of John and Liv Walton guiding us on, we are bewildered by any arrangement which is inconsistent with our dreams and our life course.

Not only are we bewildered, we are threatened. For some reason, we have an ideal of what a relationship must be in order to be valid. That ideal frequently places sex in the position of primary importance. Some of us insist that sexual fidelity is the most important criterion of love. Others insist sexual freedom is by far the most essential ingredient.

When the person with whom we have entered a primary relationship violates or threatens our position on sex, we more often than not decide to end it all and seek out another person who will adhere to our rules.

John and David and Peter and Mark are criticized for their relationships by those persons who want their own relationships to be monogamous. Why? What is so threatening about the ability of other persons to find happiness in their lives? John and David and Peter and Mark tell me that they feel a peace together they have never felt before. They don't walk the floor at night worrying about whether or not the other person *really* loves them. They don't throw up from the fear that the lover will find someone else who satisfies them more.

If I am threatened by their arrangement because it is working and it is the opposite of what I think the understanding on sex should be, I am not very secure in my ideal, my dream, my life course. Likewise, if a couple who has insisted upon an open marriage is threatened by a monogamous relationship which seems to be working, they aren't very secure with their concept of relationship.

What is an *ideal* relationship? It depends upon *your* ideal. Ideals change with growth. Perception must change with discovery. Does that mean our earlier ideals were silly? Not at all. They represented where we were and we have to be true to where we are. Does that mean that when our ideals change, we have to change partners? Perhaps, but I would hate to think so. If you and your lover entered your relationship after honestly communicating (the key word) your ideals and if you shared experiences and grew together, chances are that your ideals would have changed together. If they haven't, they may with time.

A couple who enter an open relationship, for instance, may with time decide they prefer to be monogamous. The opposite is also true. And with time, the question of sex will probably be placed in its proper perspective.

If having a consistent sex partner is all a relationship is about, it would be smarter to find a young whore. The price of services rendered couldn't possibly match the amount that goes into room, board, gifts, vacations and so on.

If, on the other hand, your ideal relationship is based on deep love; if your dream is to share yourself as a friend and companion with another; if your life course is to grow and discover, be sick and healthy, rich and poor in the company of a particular one whose devotion and whose growth prompt an internal peace, then seek out a person who shares your ideal, and don't settle for less. Sex will take its appropriate place.

♦

LIFE'S
REAL MEANING

February 1981

My ninety-year-old grandmother explained over the bridge table the other night the reason she seemed peculiarly distracted. Tuesday would be her sixty-eighth wedding anniversary. Each year since Gramps' death, Gram has spent an unplanned week in reflection on the sixty years they shared. Many of the days are teary. She misses him. On some occasions, though, you can get her laughing by asking her to recall a few of the events in their lives together. On the night of their honeymoon, for instance, the band with which Gramps played clarinet showed up outside of the hotel for a surprise serenade. "Gramps had me stand at the window and wave," she says with a smile and waving gesture, "so that he could sneak out the back door to buy cigars for the boys."

Last night, my partner, Ray, and I saw a film in which a brilliant professor decides to separate from his wife and children because he sees their seven-year marriage standing in his way of doing something meaningful with his life. He seeks to know the ultimate truth of existence and feels that his wife, children, dinner parties and household chores are all roadblocks to discovering the true meaning of life.

From time to time, I catch myself looking at Ray and wondering about our spending the next fifty-five years together. Most of the time, the thought is a delight. Once in a while, though, it frightens me.

It frightens me when I fear I may have made a mistake. The thought of spending the rest of my life with Ray scares me when I imagine I am possibly being held back from discovering the real me; that my potential to write the great American novel or replace Phil Donahue is being sapped by my commitment to Ray and my daily routine of walking and feeding the dog, tending to the canary, listening for the rinse cycle, periodically checking on the spaghetti sauce and watching *Little House on the Prairie*. I fear growing fat rather than wiser. I wonder whether this relationship will enable me to have the best mind, the best soul, the best body, the best income, the best sex, the best time I can have *or* would I be my best alone or with someone else?

I suspect those fears put me in the company of a lot of other people, including Ray. Surely, my grandfather entertained doubts from time to time too. I think the doubts are a normal part of a developing relationship. Yet, some people, gay and straight, suggest that these doubts are a good reason to avoid making commitments to another. They see them as inevitable. They feel that no one person can totally meet all of your needs, so why limit yourself to one person. Grandma's sixty years of marriage is seen by them as more of a tragedy than a cause for celebration.

Most people today, I believe, enter relationships for primarily the same reasons. We seek intimacy and security. We seek relief of the fear of loneliness. The human experience of love is rooted in human need. We long to be affirmed completely by another person. We long to be understood, cared for, respected. We say we do it for love, but *real* love is the fruit of, not the reason for, entering relationships.

Grandma and Grandpa's first few years, like Ray's and mine, were undoubtedly marked by excitement and enthusiasm. During the period of infatuation, we are blinded to the other's faults and we dream without question of total, unending commitment. We feel complete. One day, the magic wears off. Boredom leads to demands; demands prompt distance; distance encourages doubt. One or both of the lovers begin to silently and then publicly confront the other's faults. This new honesty is threatening and hurtful. Each responds by encouraging more distance. Soon, the doubts begin to dominate. "Did he really love me all of this time or did he love his image of me?" And, "He's changed. That's not the man I married!" It is at this point that many relationships end in bitterness and frustration.

It is this experience of disappointment, perhaps encountered over and over again, which prompts some people to angrily denounce relationships and to publicly deny their need for intimacy. Yet, it is fully human to seek intimacy and some hungry people express that need by an anxious preoccupation with genital encounters.

Of those people who have stayed in relationships after the end of infatuation, some have done so because of cultural or religious sanctions, because of a sense of responsibility to the children or because they were afraid to be alone. Many of these individuals spend the rest of their lives isolated, angry and regretting their decision to marry.

Other people, however—and I hope to be one of them—discover that the new honesty is eventually liberating and that the true fruits of relationship have yet to be tasted. While before there was a need to be perfect, now there is the freedom to be yourself and to explore new possibilities. While before there were demands for joint pleasure, now there is a realization that both parties are individuals, alone in the world and responsible for their own happiness. Rather than continuing to feel attacked by the other's honesty, we grow to experience their acceptance and affirmation of us as the flawed persons we all are. Rather than feeling betrayed by our awareness of the lover's faults, we are energized by our ability to love maturely all that which is imperfect.

I look forward to the future because I believe that as Ray's and my relationship grows more mature, I will learn to confidently celebrate my individuality; that I will be energized to give myself more completely to others; that I will let go of my need to be in control. When Ray and I first got together, we described relationship as a means of enabling each other to grow to our full potential. Somewhere along the line, like most everyone else, we lost sight of our goal and began to function as one entity. Mature love encourages individual growth in the presence of one who is patient, forgiving and supportive. The essence of a mature love relationship is mutual respect.

At the end of the movie we saw last night, the professor comes face to face with the soul of existence. The secret, he says, is that there is no secret. The one thing in his life which saves him from meaninglessness is his relationship with his wife. Without love, he discovers he is nothing.

Whether or not I write the great American novel or replace Donahue is irrelevant. Successes don't make life successful. I think the essence of life is learning how to love. For me, at this point in my development, that means making a commitment to Ray, walking and feeding the dog, tending to the canary, listening for the rinse cycle, periodically checking on the spaghetti sauce and watching *Little House on the Prairie*. For Grandma, it means continuing to grow independent of Gramps and being occasionally nurtured by thoughts of the sixty years they shared.

THE LETTER
IN THE DESK

May 1984

There has been an unopened letter sitting in my desk for the last three years. It was a letter I hoped my lover, Ray, would never need to read. Written just prior to my departure for an out-of-state speaking engagement, it was my final farewell in which I attempted to communicate how much our mutual love meant to me. It seems that no matter how many times and how many ways you tell the special one you love of the way you feel, you continue to search for new words put together in a new way which will *really* capture the depth and breadth of your feelings. In the event something happened to me while away from home, I wanted Ray to have some last moment of communication with me.

I remember crying when I wrote the letter. I cried again when I opened it up today to read. This month Ray and I celebrate eight years together. I opened the letter because I was sure that it needed to be updated; because it needed to be expanded upon. According to the stages described by David McWhirter and his lover Drew Mattison in their important book, *The Male Couple—How Relationships Develop*, Ray and I are in a different stage now than we were when I wrote him my good-bye. I wanted to make sure the good-bye reflected the last three years of growth in our love.

My love for Ray and his for me are as integral to my life as breathing, it seems. The world is seen by us through our love. We celebrate the goodness of life and cope with its challenges as a couple. Most of our good friends live similarly. For that reason, I am always a bit startled when asked by a straight person, "How can two men be in a relationship?" I have to remind myself that people thought the world was flat until they sailed it.

Even more disturbing to me are the protestations by young gay men that it isn't possible for them to have a long-lasting relationship.

"Who told you that?" I will ask.

"My friends in the bar," they will say.

In the last several weeks, I have spent long evenings of discussion with lesbian and gay college students in three states. Consistently, their prime concern has been "Is it possible to have a relationship that lasts?"

It is with those college students in mind, and those others who are convinced the world is flat, that I share the thoughts from my former final farewell to Ray. Please keep in mind that this was not written for public consumption but as the private last words of one lover to another. Perhaps, though, they will serve as a signpost.

Ray, my love,

I hope that you don't open this envelope until you are 100 years old and you have just found me in my bed with a 103-year-old smile on my face, but there are no guarantees about how long we will live and I wanted you to have something extra from me after I moved on.

Be sad and cry and be happy about your tears because they will be a wonderful testimony to the exciting, growing, giving life of love we shared. Be assured that if there is any way I can make my presence felt to you, I will do so. At the very least, I will hang around as long as it is allowed.

Do with my bodily remains what you will, but at this time in my life, I would like to donate whatever is usable to medicine and have the rest burned and scattered over whatever spot has special significance to the two of us. Hold me in your memory as a happy, pleasant thought, if you will. Know that it was through you that I really felt the beauty of loving and being loved and my only regret is that I didn't spend every possible moment reminding you of my affection and devotion. But we did love well and as I have frequently said, we have much to be thankful for. (Never end a sentence with a preposition!)

My life with you was more than I ever dreamed of and when I used to get down in the dumps about the progress I was making with my work or my inability to bring in decent money, I would think about you and how lucky I was to be alive and in love.

Be open to the comforting gestures of our family and friends and be a source of strength to them too. Share with them the stories of our times with them and laugh together. If nothing else, I would like to think I had offered the gift of laughter.

If I haven't already done so, please make a point of contacting the people in my life whose actions caused me pain and those for whom my actions prompted pain in their lives. I know it is not our actions but our expectations which prompt hurtful feelings and I beg their forgiveness and offer my own.

Get Tommy to help you with my filing cabinets. Perhaps the National Gay Archives or some similar group would be interested in having my files and assorted gay-oriented materials. Give away only that which you don't wish to keep for yourself.

Whatever you do, Raymond, don't live for too long in the memories of the past. Remember me, but love again. You have too much to give; too much beauty to sit back as a spectator. Your love for another will not diminish our love one iota. You gave me 100 percent but the supply has not been depleted.

I'm sure I wasn't the easiest person in the world with whom to live, but I tried hard, and, as a teacher in high school insisted, "A saint is a sinner who tries."

If the Church should decide to begin canonization proceedings, don't discourage them! When they start looking for miracles, tell them I grew to my full potential. There is no greater miracle for a gay person today. Tell them, too, that I kept the Faith, which is also no small task. Finally (because they always look for three), tell them how we loved each other selflessly.

If I should die at the hands of a frightened person, forgive him or her for both of us. The message we have been communicating is alarming to people who are afraid of difference and terrified by change. I don't want to die in such a violent manner, but I may, and that is perhaps why I am writing all of this down. Yet, I know I won't be called before my time.

Be at peace, my love. Brian is on the roof, but the air is fresh and the view is wonderful. Thank you.

One day soon, I will write another letter to Ray and tuck it away into my desk. I suspect that I will write many final notes, every few years pulling out the last one to review and amend its contents. I also suspect that the letters will become shorter and shorter. Like God, true love defies description. The more you try to describe it, the more you limit it. Perhaps the final note will merely say, "Until later."

DESPITE IT ALL,
WE LOVE

September 1985

Jack McCarty and Victor Amburgy couldn't get seats together for the short TWA flight from Athens to Rome, but it didn't bother them much in the beginning. Later, however, as they crouched motionless and silently in their seats with their hands folded over their bowed heads, it tore their hearts apart that they couldn't see or hear, much less touch, the other. Facing probable death at the hands of two crazed Shiite hijackers, they each agonized most that they would part without being able to say good-bye.

The seventeen-day ordeal experienced by these gay lovers and the way they comforted each other privately serves as a poignant reminder to all of us that there is something very special, and indeed sacred, about the love two men or two women can have for each other. At a time when Falwell, Swaggart and Schlafly exploit the horrors of AIDS to deny the decency of gay and lesbian love, Jack and Victor, and scores of others like them, dramatically remind us of the strength and beauty which is possible for gay relationships in this world of fear and hatred.

Though separated for the entire time aboard the TWA prison, Victor and Jack were reunited in a dark and damp death wagon, used at other times to transport the dead of Beirut to the grave but now employed to cart the American hostages to secret hideaways. "It was in that awful stench," Jack told me, "that I was first able to lean over, kiss Victor on the neck and whisper 'I love you.' He, then, did the same." Had Jack and Victor been discovered in that private display of affection by their Shiite captors or been exposed by the other Americans, it could have meant immediate death, as is proscribed by Islam.

It was under similar circumstances that Jack secretly held Victor, who by then was weak from diarrhea. They were in isolation with one other American in a basement cell. In a black corner of that room they embraced, holding on for dear life.

"On more than one occasion, I stepped in to protect Victor," Jack explained. "I was somewhat of a spokesperson. The guards listened to me. I had to be very careful but fortunately, both times I fought them about Victor being removed, I won."

Unknown to Victor, Jack also offered himself as a hostage in his lover's place. It was at the end of the ordeal, but no one knew yet that the terms for release would be agreed upon. All of the hostages had privately wished at least once that death would come swiftly and end the day-to-day speculation. Finally, Jack and nine others asked the Red Cross to arrange to have them held and the remaining Americans, including Victor, freed. "The Red Cross thanked us for our gesture," Jack said, "but said it wasn't possible."

Once freed, once safe again on American soil, Jack and Victor hugged enthusiastically in front of television cameras as an astonished president and nation looked on.

Since hearing the details of Jack and Victor's experience, I have more than once imagined my lover, Ray, and me on that ill-fated flight. Like many of you, I have wondered how I would have survived hours and hours of anguished separation. I have stayed awake at night trying to figure out how I would have comforted Ray; how I would have protected him.

It is in the face of adversity, I think, that the breadth and depth of our relationships are experienced. In writing about friendship, Oscar Wilde said that he wouldn't be the least offended if a friend didn't invite him to a feast, "but if a friend of mine had a sorrow and refused to allow me to share it, I should feel it most bitterly. If he shut the doors of the house of mourning against me, I would move back again and again and beg to be admitted so that I might share in what I was entitled to share."

It is no coincidence that these wise words on the essence of friendship, which is the basis of all true love relationships, came from the soul of a gay man. Wilde's words, as well as Jack and Victor's story, serve as poignant examples to everyone of the strength and beauty of love between two men. And there are other examples.

Throughout this country, thousands of gay men are sitting at the bedsides and holding the weakened hands of their gay lovers and friends. In an atmosphere which is often hostile and often hysteric, these men are heroically battling the fears and depressions of their lovers, their in-laws and themselves in their attempt to bring hope, dignity and comfort to an often desperate situation. For some of these men, that man that lies in the hospital bed or on the couch at home has been an essential part of their dreams for many, many years. For other men, their allegiance is to a man they met just prior to his AIDS diagnosis. And some of these gay men who are building loving friendships with persons with AIDS had never met the man before being assigned as his buddy.

In some parts of this country, the gay man at the side of the bed holds his lover's hand boldly and defiantly. For others, the small town has an atmosphere not unlike that of Beirut and the signs of affection are done with daring. In so many of the circumstances, the healthy survivor, as Jack, asks if he might be taken instead.

In less dramatic but nonetheless critical fashion, the gay and lesbian lovers of alcoholics are often asked to test their love and commitment. A world of dreams in the process of being fulfilled can turn into a nightmare with a "slip," and each lover is called upon to believe in the strength of the relationship and to recommit himself or herself to the journey they are making together.

On a day-to-day basis, gay and lesbian relationships endure all of the challenges, big and small, which are thrown at all couples, such as changes in employment, moving out of town, depression, economic stress, automobile accidents, sickness, hostile in-laws, infatuation with others, clogged drains, broken heirlooms, impotence, midlife crisis, the wrong bid in bridge, burnt toast, loss of custody and ring around the collar. We generally do this without the support of the Church, the state, family or the neighbors.

The pressures placed upon gay men and lesbians to be straight, to be celibate or to be quiet are more than are ever placed on any heterosexual relationship. Particularly at this frightening time of rapid growth in intolerant religious fundamentalism, right-wing fanaticism and AIDS hysteria, the obstacles to loving another person of the same gender with determination, loyalty, caring and celebration are enormous. Yet, despite it all, we love.

Despite the closet, we love. Despite the Crusades, we love. Despite the Inquisition, we love. Despite the witch-hunts and trials, we love. Despite the Holocaust, we love. Despite Joseph McCarthy, we love. Despite Jerry Falwell, Jimmy Swaggart and Phyllis Schlafly, we love. Despite crazed Shiites, we love. Despite the horrors of AIDS, we love. Despite everything they say about us and do to us, we love. Despite everything, we love and we love well.

THE JOURNEY
FORWARD

THE JOURNEY
FORWARD

The time can come in the life of a gay man or lesbian woman when the decision is made to move on; to let go of the need to be accommodated and to embrace the invitation to be in charge of life. The time comes more than once, but once it comes and once you take the first step on the journey forward, it's hard to backstep into a position where someone else's acceptance of you determines whether you like yourself. Gay and lesbian Christians and Jews have to battle hard to step forward because they are encouraged from all sides to give up control of their spirituality. It is no small task to be within the Church without backstepping, and its no small task to be outside of the Church and to journey forward without the support of community. The trick is in understanding that serenity is the goal and that you achieve serenity not from others' approval but from within your soul. When your self-worth is nonnegotiable, you can be inside or outside any of society's structures. It doesn't matter. Serenity comes when you are in charge of the journey forward.

THE SAD
DILEMMA OF
THE GAY
CATHOLIC

August 1975

With the black sleeves of his religious habit shoved halfway up his hairy arms, the small finger of his left hand busily picking wax out of his ear, Brother made quite clear to the senior honors religion class what the position of the church is on homosexuality.

"If you come into my office and tell me that you have shacked up with some broad," announced the school's senior guidance counselor, occasionally eyeing the wax on his little finger, "I'll talk to you. But if you tell me you're queer, I'll kick you out of the office."

Officially, the position of the Roman Catholic Church is that homosexual orientation is in itself not sinful, but the expression of it is gravely sinful.

Yet, upon admission of his or her orientation, the homosexual is kicked not only out of the guidance office in the Catholic high school, but out of the pulpit, seminary, convent, monastery, charismatic prayer group, place of employment, home, apartment, family and circle of friends. Homosexuals, upon confession or discovery, are kicked out of the Christian community until such time as they admit their illness and seek the cure of a psychiatrist or equally misguided priest.

Because of its roots and its history, because of its size and its influence, the Roman Catholic Church is seen by the gay community as the southern white racist of the black-white struggle; as the male chauvinist pig of the female-male struggle; as the bullying Teamster of the UFW-Teamster struggle.

With roots in the Jewish tradition, Christians are the adopted children of sexist bias and sexual taboos—biases and taboos which are unexamined in light of the law of love.

Sodom and Gomorrah, Leviticus, St. Paul's letters to the Romans and Corinthians seem proof of God's disgust with homosexuals.

But modern Scripture scholars insist Sodom and Gomorrah has nothing to do with homosexuality. The legendary destruction of the cities was brought about by the wickedness and perhaps inhospitality of the people. In the sixteen references in Scripture to the Genesis 19 account, there is not one support that the fire and brimstone which hailed from heaven came as the result of homosexual love.

Those persons who quickly quote Leviticus and that book's condemnation of men lying with men had best read the entire law and be amused at the variety of violations we all merrily incur daily. Those who pick and choose what they wish to quote should read Leviticus 11:9–12 the next time they sit down to lobster or New England clam chowder.

Jewish condemnation (death by stoning) of homosexuality and sodomy (anal intercourse) did not surface until after the Babylonian captivity. Until that time, there was no law against same-sex lovemaking. But the race of people that was small in size and threatened constantly by larger tribes and races began protecting itself by insisting that all sexual activity have procreation as its end.

Men could not lie with men because they wasted the seed of procreation—the only means of increasing the numbers of the Jewish people. There is, oddly enough, no law against women lying with women. But that may also reveal the Jewish attitude toward the importance of women.

It has also been suggested that the condemnation of sodomy—an act which can be and is performed by both heterosexual and homosexual couples—is the response of a degraded people to a practice which was used by their Babylonian captors as a visible sign of supremacy. Sodomy is used synonymously with homosexuality under the supposition that all homosexuals engage in anal intercourse. The supposition is false.

Homosexual prostitution, the third source of Jewish condemnation, was so closely identified with idolatry (Ashtoreth and Baal) in the Jewish mind that the terms were often interchangeable—condemnation of one was condemnation of the other—much like the late Senator McCarthy's association of homosexuality and treason.

As a group of monotheists in a world dominated by polytheists, the Jews condemned anything associated with the worship of false gods. Into this culture was born Saul of Tarsus, a good Jew whose zeal for the Faith brought forth a new testament of beautiful writings, inspired by the teachings of the Messiah. But Paul's writings also reveal his Jewish bias in the areas of women and sex and his own personal "thorn in the flesh" hangups in others.

It is with the Pauline writings that Christians are most inconsistent. Few today will quote Paul when he advises men to cut their hair short and women to cover their heads and be subject to their husbands. Even the most dedicated celibate will water down Paul's incredible approach to marriage and sex.

But who holds back a single syllable when the man writes his condemnation of the homosexual? St. Paul is divinely inspired. Surely he speaks for God!

Without such Scriptural criticism, however, the church went forward, guided by Christ's beautiful message of love (a message which incidentally never mentions homosexuality) and burdened by a reactionary tradition of legalism, sexism and a contempt of the flesh.

The first formal legislation against the homosexual in the church (in which pederasts were denied last rites), according to John Lauritsen in his *Religious Roots of the Taboo on Homosexuality*, was enacted at the Council of Elvira A.D. 300.

As with all other abuses, the sufferings began worldwide for the homosexual when Christianity was declared the state religion by Constantine in the early fourth century.

In A.D. 342, a decree imposed the death penalty for sodomy. In 390, Emperor Valentian initiated death by burning, in the tradition of Sodom and Gomorrah.

An edict of Theodosius banned all religions other than Christianity. Loyalty to the state, according to Lauritsen, demanded loyalty to the laws of the Faith, including the code of sexual morality. Heresy equaled treason. Soon after, homosexuality was seen as heresy, which in turn, was a treasonous offense.

In 538, Justinian codified the Roman law and subsequently prescribed torture, mutilation, and castration for homosexuals.

Justinian's *Novella 77* blames homosexuality for famines, earthquakes, and pestilences. Sodomites, as they were called, were put to death, lest the entire city and its inhabitants perish.

Justinian's *Novella 141* speaks of homosexuality as ". . . such as have gone to decay through the abominable and impious conduct deservedly hated by God."

The effect of Justinian's policies is summed up in *Phallos*, by Thorkil Vanggaard, who states:

> Thus what was originally an exclusively Jewish attitude towards homosexuality and phallic symbolism had gained ascendancy over the whole Christian world. A true Christian believer was marked out from then on by his unconditional condemnation of everything homosexual. Correspondingly, homosexual acts were regarded as unshakeable proof of heterodoxy.

During the Dark Ages, homosexuals were punished by the church with excommunication, denial of last rites, castration, torture, mutilation, death by burning and burial in unsanctified ground. Some church fathers, from fear of "pollution," also insisted that the corpses be mutilated.

As the church began waging battle on heretics throughout Europe, slaughtering thousands under the sign of the Cross, so too did it gleefully dispose of any living creature who was suspected of being a homosexual. Heresy and homosexuality were inseparable.

"During the Middle Ages, heretics were accused of unnatural vice as a matter of course," writes Westermarck in *Origin and Development of Moral Ideas.* "Indeed, so closely was sodomy associated with heresy that the same name was applied to both." In the thirteenth century, St. Thomas Aquinas insisted "right reason declares the appointed end of sexual acts is procreation." In the tradition of his predecessor Augustine, Aquinas viewed homosexuality as an evil because the acts could not result in procreation. They were, therefore, *peccata contra naturam* (sins against nature).

Aquinas even went so far as to assert that masturbation was more evil than forcible rape and incest, reasoning that rape and incest could result in blessed procreation. Masturbation, obviously, could not.

Sodomy, by the Middle Ages, was referred to as *peccatum illud horribile inter Christianos non nominandum*—the sin so horrible that it must not be mentioned in the presence of Christians. Those who question the influence of the church would do well to check the English criminal law where they will find the same wording used into the nineteenth century.

The term *faggot*, a favorite term of opprobrium, owes its origin to the Roman Catholic Church. A faggot was a measure of sticks which were bundled together for burning . . . most often for the incineration of a heretic.

From the Oxford English Dictionary comes the explanation, "With special reference to the practice of burning heretics alive, especially in phrase 'fire and faggot,' and to 'fry a faggot'; to be burned alive."

The Inquisition delighted in burning faggots. "Homosexuality in the Middle Ages," according to historian Henry Kamen, "was treated as the ultimate crime against morality, and the standard definitions of it refer to the 'abominable' or the 'unspeakable' crime. . . . The usual punishment was burning alive." *(The Spanish Inquisition.)*

When Protestants went their own way, most often leaving behind what they considered the evil thinking and practices of the Roman Church, they generally carried with them the sexual code of condemnation. Henry VIII in England and the Cal-

vinists in Amsterdam continued the legacy of homosexual anni-
hilation.

It wasn't until 1861 that the death penalty was removed in
England for sodomy. In Scotland it remained the practice until
1889. Homosexuals in Nazi Germany were shot without trial or
sent by the thousands to extermination in Hitler's infamous con-
centration camps.

This all took place proudly under the banner of the Judeo-
Christian ethic. No antihomosexual taboo existed in China,
Japan, India, the Arab countries or pre-Columbian America.

Even today, in 1975, homosexual activity is a punishable
offense in nearly every state in this country. In some states, the
punishment is life imprisonment. In others, homosexuals are
sent to state hospitals where they are given shock treatment and
vomiting-inducing chemicals, as in *A Clockwork Orange*, to convert their behavior to a more acceptable pattern of sexual response. The therapy is overwhelmingly unsuccessful and
psychologically destructive, but it continues all the same.

What hurts the Catholic homosexual who loves the Church
and who tries to live a life based on Christ's selfless law of love,
is that the unchallenged champion of oppression against the gay
community is still the Roman Catholic Church.

The main headline of the May 24, 1974, *New York Times*
reads, "Council, by 22–19, Defeats Bill on Homosexual Rights
. . . Opposition by Archdiocese Cited as Key Factor on Vote."

"It was the opposition of the Roman Catholic Archdiocese
of New York," the *Times* article read, "that most politicians cite
as the key factor in the defeat of the measure which would have
banned discrimination in housing, jobs or public accommoda-
tions because of 'sexual preference.'"

The bill sought only to guarantee the homosexual the right
to live where he or she wanted to live and to work where he or
she wanted to work. The bill said nothing about the moral
rightness or wrongness of being a homosexual.

In this post-Vatican II era, the Roman Catholic Church has
prided itself in the often late but strong defense of the oppressed. Blacks and Chicanos have a friend and ally in the Roman Catholic Church. Even women are beginning to make some
headway in an institution as sexist as Hugh Hefner.

But with a group of people estimated to be twenty million

strong in this country, a group which has one of the highest suicide rates among oppressed people, a group the *Wall Street Journal* refers to as our "last minority," the Roman Catholic Church leads the battle in Goliath fashion against even those who seek to remain faithful.

". . . within a few days, a front-page editorial in *The Catholic News*, the official newspaper of the New York Archdiocese, labeled the measure a threat to family life and urged its opposition," the *Times* reported.

"The church action prompted a torrent of mail and of opposition resolutions from neighborhood groups—veterans' posts, Holy Name Societies and civic organizations—that put the bill in trouble."

Similar action and opposition was equally successful in Worcester, Massachusetts, and Philadelphia. In both cities, the church sought to save the people from "pollution."

But the oppression of gays is not always blatant enough to make headlines. Most every day, Catholic homosexuals feel far more subtle forms of blind, ignorant persecution.

The homosexual penitent, for instance, is advised, through the direction of the National Conference of Catholic Bishops, that celibacy is his or her calling. All homosexuals by virtue of their orientation (of which they had no choice) are called to a life of sexual abstinence in the eyes of the Church.

"I haven't been to the sacraments in 15 years," writes one man. "How do you reconcile your sexuality with your Faith? Do you receive Communion?" "My confessor tells me that I am living in sin," confides another. "He insists that I report to him every Saturday."

"My friend is a convert to the Faith. He is gay but because he wants to be a priest he has announced that he hates homosexuals. What do I do for him?"

"I am a nun. I have loved another nun for 12 years. Is there anything you can say to us that will help us to understand how God views us?"

Perhaps the most disturbing question came from a friend, a former Franciscan, who, after sharing in the Liturgy, took me aside and asked in all sincerity, "Brian, do you think we are really going to hell?"

Living in a secret world for as long as they can remember,

homosexuals are forced to be islands unto themselves. Childish fears and fantasies and a million unanswered questions are kept penned up within. Communication is impossible; sharing too threatening.

Where, for instance, does the male homosexual turn when at age fourteen he is more attracted to the foldout in *Playgirl* than he is to the one in *Playboy?*

Whom does he confide in at age eighteen after having had his first sexual encounter with another human being?

How does a man explain that he has fallen in love with another man to heterosexual friends and relatives? Worse yet, where and to whom does he go when he has lost his first love and aches inside as he has never ached before?

His Mom and Dad? Sister Mary? Brother Duffy? Msgr. McPhillips? His doctor? His friends?

The horror stories of gay men and women are consistent in revealing the same treatment over and over again when they dared to share with a straight person their homosexuality.

One young man was called outside the confessional, where he was promptly decked by the priest-confessor. Another tells of how the priest went to the parents of his friend and insisted their son not be allowed to continue the friendship.

Some parents have been known to order their children out of the house until their orientation changes. Others smile sympathetically as they wildly leaf through the phone book looking desperately for a psychiatrist.

Upon sharing his orientation with his charismatic prayer group, one Detroit gay was told to either submit himself to the healing power of the group or never come back. "Praise the Lord, we love you brother, but God says in Genesis 19 . . ."

For that reason, the phone calls and letters pour in.

"I am 15. I read about you in the paper and I wondered if maybe you could introduce me to someone. I'm really lonely."

"I'm married . . . have been for 12 years. I have a son, but I'm not happy. I'm not gay if I'm married, right? Then why do I feel the way I do?"

"I'm 84 and for the majority of my life I have been a prisoner of fear. I pray that what you are doing will free others who follow to live freely."

Live freely? Ultimately it is the decision of the individual.

And it is called "coming out" in the gay community. It means accepting one's homosexuality and sharing that orientation with family, friends and working cohorts. The degree to which the homosexual can do that determines the degree of his or her freedom. But always there is a price. The greater the freedom, the greater the price.

My freedom began only after twenty-five years of hiding, of keeping my secret, of being what others thought I ought to be.

"Who are you taking to the prom, Brian?" "I saw Sarah Murphy's mother the other day. She said Sarah's home. Why don't you ask her out?" "Hey, McNaught, how many broads have you had?" "That one ought to be married. He'd make a fine father."

The nightmare ended with a bottle of paint thinner. With tears flowing freely in the emergency room at St. Joe's Hospital—a tube down my throat pumping out my stomach—I promised myself that I would never again live for the whims and expectations of other human beings.

This promise was not an easy one for me. After the local newspaper identified me as a homosexual and as president of the local chapter of Dignity—a national organization of gay Catholics—my column in a diocesan newspaper, in which I had previously defended Christian gay love, was dropped.

The editors said they eliminated my column because of space limitations, though I find it difficult to believe this was the real reason.

Later I began a public fast and was subsequently fired as a staff writer for the diocesan newspaper. The editors claimed I had terminated my own contract.

Until the headlines about my case hit the local press last year, homosexuality was not something commonly discussed in the chancery. As one bishop confessed to me, "I have read more about homosexuality in the last week than I have in my entire ministry."

So while the incident was a personal hardship for me, there were some ensuing events which, I think, are a sign of hope for both gay Catholics and the Church. It might be helpful to look at these.

After my column was dropped, a conference of gay Catholic activists and sympathizers was organized. It was to be a study weekend which included a Mass of solidarity and a silent, peaceful march to the chancery "to give visible witness to the belief that the love of God extends to all persons, regardless of sexual orientation, guaranteeing for them the right to the pursuit of happiness and the Christian ideal."

Perhaps because the conference was opposed by the archbishop (who described gay people in a letter as those with "arrested sexual development") or perhaps because heterosexual Catholics can't afford to be mistaken as gay, the turnout was smaller than the organizers had hoped. But the clergy and religious who did attend were an important source of hope to the assembled community.

One of them, veteran humanitarian Msgr. Clement Kern, said, "All of us, gay and straight alike, have come here today to affirm ourselves before God in faith; to accept ourselves without regrets or self-pity; and to seek a good and full life in keeping with our potential for growth and God's call.

"We especially regret the misconceptions, taboos, biases and fears which are directed at our gay brothers and sisters. If growing to sexual maturity is difficult for straight people, the constant barrage of ridicule, ignorance and condemnation which falls on gay people demands that their efforts at growth be almost superhuman."

And yet there are more homosexuals than most people think, and they tend to be as well-adjusted, productive, and as interested in pursuing traditional ideals as any group. Homosexuality is not chosen. It, like heterosexuality, is the result of a variety of conditions, probably both psychological and physical. Many homosexuals are as intent upon settling down with one person as are heterosexuals. And statistically, their relationships last as long.

The American Psychiatric Association virtually admitted that homosexuality is not a disease when it voted unanimously in 1973 to remove homosexuality from the diagnostic and statistical manual of psychiatric disorders.

Unfortunately, the myths and stereotypes about homosexuals rather than the new attitude of the American Psychiatric Association seem to be more characteristic of the Church. So it was the task of the weekend conference to find a way to communicate with an institution which seemed to refuse to listen. Does one picket? Write a letter to the editor? Ask for an audience with the bishop?

For me, the only authentic, nonviolent, Christian method was a prayerful fast. No food. No drink. Scripturally, it seemed a sound vehicle of communication, of calling attention to an evil, of making reparation for what I saw as a grave sin on the part of the Church.

"As a man who loves his Church and as a gay who loves his gay brothers and sisters," my fast statement said, "I am in daily torment.

"Fully believing in the mission of my Church to bring all persons into the Divine Presence through the example of the selfless love of Jesus, I embrace my Faith and the community of believers and dedicate myself to that goal.

"Fully sharing in the normal sexual orientation of my gay brothers and sisters, I am led by the same natural human drives for creative loving union with a person of my choosing, regardless of gender.

"But my love for my Church and my love for my gay brothers and sisters are in conflict. My Church does not love my gay brothers and sisters. My Church unscrupulously persecutes them. This I can no longer tolerate spiritually, physically, or emotionally."

My fast lasted twenty-four days, seventeen of which were on water. It took those twenty-four days, twenty-four pounds, and mostly sleepless nights, before the Church responded.

The two auxiliary bishops who were in town at the time delivered a letter to us:

"From the outset, let us say that we respect the motives behind your fast and the sincerity of your efforts. . . .

"The gift of sexuality deserves deeper understanding and appreciation than has often been given in our society and in our church. Some efforts toward continuing education in this regard have been made. A priests' workshop on sexuality is being planned for the near future and we, on our part, will support it fully. We will urge that special attention be given to the question of homosexuality. . . .

"While the Catholic Church, in view of its moral teaching, cannot endorse or condone overt homosexual acts, we have a

serious obligation to root out structures and attitudes that discriminate against the homosexual as a person. We will exert our leadership in behalf of this effort.

"We hope for your continued cooperation with us in trying to achieve this goal."

There were some who were disappointed with the letter and with my decision to end the fast. However, those of us who had dealt with the Church in this and in other areas over the years knew that we had received more than met the eye.

Catholic gays want to stay within the Church. As much as anyone else, they love their cultural heritage and the guiding challenge of the Faith. The Mass and the Sacraments and the Nicene Creed are as rich in meaning for the Catholic homosexual as they are for the Catholic heterosexual.

No one should have expected the bishops to issue a public statement reversing two thousand years of procreative theology. If such a reversal comes, it will begin with theologians. But the bishops pledged an effort at education, and where there is the pursuit of education, there is the pursuit of truth.

Homosexuals cannot be hurt by truth. Only helped.

✦

BUT DO
YOU LOVE
THE CHURCH?

Winter 1980

The wrinkled brow across the breakfast table belonged to a
well-to-do Catholic who had, from time to time, financially supported my efforts for reconciliation with the Church in the past
and was now listening to me wrestle with defeat.

As an admirer and previous backer of Boston street priest
Paul Shanley, my friend came to town to talk with us about the
national retreat house we were promoting for lesbians, gay men
and their families. Prior to that meeting, he and I sat together,
sipped Sanka and exchanged family and Church news.

The night before he had dined with his bishop; the Saturday prior he had donned overalls to paint a Catholic home he
had helped build for unwed mothers. Diligently spiritual and
delightfully simple, he loves his Church—our Church. He cher-
ishes his parochial education and laments that his daughters no
longer find Mass meaningful. His charitable concerns range
from being frequent honorary director of diocesan fundraising
to secretly seeking funds to help alcoholic bishops and clergy.
As long as it is for the Church and for people who seek to be

part of the Church, it commands his attention. For that reason, he was greatly distressed as I talked of my work as a gay Catholic as being "a battle with despair."

Earlier, we had shared our major disappointment with the Pope, with the treatment of Hans Kung and Bill Callahan and with the seeming capitulation of the Dutch hierarchy. Sensing his loyalty didn't suggest blindness, I began to build my case for frustration. I told him the horror stories of seminary witch-hunts, about murdered gay clergy and religious and about the hypocrisy of closeted bishops. I mocked the Vatican Catch 22 position that homosexuals are incapable of embracing celibacy but must be celibate. I shared with him the intense bitterness of former Catholics who now hate God because the clergy have taught them God hates them. I recalled the telephone conversation I had with an anonymous medical student who desperately sought to speak with a sympathetic priest before he died of an overdose and how we couldn't find one available. ("What happened to him? I don't know. He hung up.") Because I knew he cared, I opened the dam and let gush forth my personal pain, anger and discouragement and that of my gay Christian friends.

"But you still love the Church, don't you?" he asked with eyes stretched open and eyebrows cocked expectantly.

For years the answer has been prompt, though not always easy. "Of course I love the Church," I would respond. "The Church is the people who seek to live the Gospel. I love the Gospel. I love the people. You and I are being used by the Spirit to renew the Church."

My heart ached with anxiety. My facial muscles quivered in confusion. He had asked the question I didn't want asked at that moment. Maybe next month, maybe next week, maybe even tomorrow, but not today. Today I am afraid of my response. Today I feel like the son of a highly respected community leader who secretly beats her child. Today my pain is stronger than my devotion. Today I can't find the words to defend my parent against the curses of the neighbors and relatives who know. Today I fear I will stand rigid and scream "I hate the Church! I hate it! I hate it!"

But I didn't stand before my friend and scream. I sat paralyzed by guilt. I was immobilized by a secret sense of failure. I smiled weakly. It was enough of a yes to get by on. Sometimes, that's all I have.

There was a time, I explained, when I drew some strength from imagining myself watching the Pope, the bishops and certain pompous members of the clergy being confronted by God on the Final Day with all of the physical and spiritual anguish they caused lesbians, gay men and their families; confronted, like Hitler, with the wailing of homosexuals for all eternity. Today, my theology has changed, leaving me without the satisfaction of knowing I will watch the mighty fall.

"Gee," he said, hoping to brighten things up a bit, "I'm kind of banking on a heaven and hell and on encountering a God who will grant me eternal reward for bringing one person to the Church. That's what I've always been told," he said. "All you had to do to be saved was bring one soul back to the Church."

"And I'm afraid," I replied, "that my bringing one gay person back to the Church where I know he or she will be brutalized might be my ticket to your 'hell.'"

A Trappist monk friend of mine suggests that I should have stood and screamed "I hate the Church." When I finished with that, he said, I "should stand and scream 'I hate God! I hate God!'" Until that happens, he said, I will have a child-parent relationship to both my Church and my God.

"There are three major crises in our lives," he said. "The first is when we discover our father isn't perfect. The second is when we discover the Church isn't holy. The third is when we realize Jesus isn't a magician. Until we enter these crises, we can't know the meaning of true love or true faith."

Long ago, I discovered my father's flaws and hated him for them. Now we are friends. The Jesuits were quick to make clear to me the fragile qualities of the traditional Jesus image, and after feeling angry for being tricked, I can now love him as a brother. The Church, however, has a greater hold on me than either my father or Jesus. The Church has demanded total love and complete obedience. While my father and Jesus called me to adulthood, the Church has shielded me from reality, discouraged me from growing, forbidden me to be myself.

Gay Christians must admit their hatred of the Church before they can approach the Church as adults. Until we are able to stand rigid and scream out our anger, we will continue to be children who clamor for love and acceptance and who throw tantrums when we don't get it. Until we are able to believe that we are the Church, we will continue to bore adult Christians with our adolescent stories of what the bishop did to his priest secretary.

"But do you still love the Church?!"

Not yet. I'm not finished being angry.

DUPLICITY

Summer 1979

A letter arrived a few days ago from "the large Episcopalian who brought his own lunch" to a recent speaking engagement of mine in Miami. "I am writing to you," he said, "to share some sadness and some anger. . . . A friend of mine was murdered last week.

"He was a very closeted gay priest, vicar of a small mission. . . . He had been there eight years and was deeply loved by his congregation. The church secretary found his nude body, hands tied behind his back; his head had been beaten with a hammer.

"There are speculations about a young drifter who was taken in by the vicar and of course gossip about what may have happened. Whatever did happen may never be known, but what has disturbed me almost as much about his death is the way people have been reacting to it."

The letter then described an incredible conspiracy of silence by his friends, gay and straight, and by the local church. I say "incredible" but it wasn't at all. Undoubtedly, it was the fear of such a predictable reaction of raised eyebrows, deep sighs and silence which forced the vicar to remain in the closet in the first place. It was the fear of public scorn which prompted him to take foolish chances with a disturbed drifter so that he might know some warmth of human intimacy, no matter how limited. Surely it was the sinfully distorted image of homo-sexuality, prompted by ignorance and perpetuated by silence, which filled the head of whoever it was who so mercilessly mur-dered the priest.

Since receiving the letter, I have agonized over my own role in the death of the vicar. Am I silent at times when my voice would help eliminate the kind of self-hate which prompts people to seek comfort in dangerous settings? Am I too polite in my political stance with the Church? Two events within the week intensified the emotional and spiritual wrestling match.

The Boston media ran the story of a Catholic Brother, studying for the priesthood, whose throat was slashed from ear to ear and who was stabbed in the back, chest and hand. A closeted homosexual, he, too, sought human contact, drove in from out of state (to protect himself), picked up a stranger, per-formed sexually and was murdered. He was found outside the motel room (a half-hour after registering under a phony name) when other guests were awakened by his screams. More raised eyebrows, deep sighs and silence.

About the same time the Episcopal vicar was buried, an-other funeral of an ordained Christian minister, also a closeted homosexual, was taking place up north. There were no raised eyebrows or deep sighs at this man's wake. He was considered a great priest, a Prince of the Church, a leading defender of the Faith. Nor was there silence. His life prompted long and enthu-siastic testimonies. Besides, none of his many hundreds of mourners knew he was a homosexual.

There is a direct correlation between the lives, deaths and funerals of these three men beyond the fact that all three were active homosexuals, ordained Christian ministers (or an aspi-rant) and fearfully silent about their sexual orientation. There is a connection between the mute consent of the respected bishop when his brother bishops publicly condemned homosexuality as a serious disorder and the violent deaths of the vicar and the Brother; a corollary between the image of heterosexual pro-priety which all three, like thousands of other homosexual clergy, attempted to maintain and the self-righteous viciousness of the two murders.

I have known for some time that the celebrated bishop, like various other members of the hierarchy, was a homosexual and for that reason feel that I, too, share in the death of the vicar and the Brother. Perhaps if I and others had not protected the bishop, the Church might have more aggressively tackled the issue and set about the task of educating its people. Perhaps if we privately confronted those bishops who publicly oppose civil rights for gays, legislation would finally pass and attitudes would change. Perhaps we gay Christians share the responsibility for our oppression.

The emphasis is on the word *perhaps*. For that reason my days are filled with prayers for guidance, long discussions with other gay Christians and strategy debates with other activists. The other side of the question became clear to me on a television talk show five years ago. Jeannine Gramick and I were debating Kenneth Baker, an ultraconservative Jesuit theologian who condemned me to hell. When I suggested there was a higher percentage of homosexuality in the clergy than in the general population and that included members of the hierarchy, Baker turned beet red. "Name one!" he snapped. "Name just one!" "No," I said, "were I to mention names, you would try to do the same thing to those men that the Church in Detroit has done to me."

When I began working at the diocesan newspaper nine years ago, I became privy to information flowing through the Catholic grapevine—that network of journalists, priests, religious and middle-management laity whose loose lips have never sunk a holy vessel but whose firsthand tidbits do make life as a Church member much more interesting. For the last several years, most of the data to reach my ears has been about who is and who isn't homosexual among the clergy. Throughout this time, most especially when I was working with Dignity National, I wrestled with myself and with other gay Christians about the ethics involved in our policital struggle. Should we be confronting the churches with the information; with the hypocrisy of their position? The debate became most intense on those occasions when seminarians were expelled by closeted rectors, when official documents were released and when certain bishops announced they would go to jail rather than hire a homosexual.

Yet, always we deferred. It would be dirty politics, we thought. It's slander. What if we're wrong? It isn't fair to the individual. We had better keep our noses clean if we hope to have future dialogues with the hierarchy.

In 1976, Richard Ginder, the highly controversial Pittsburgh priest who authored *Binding with Briars—Sex and Sin in the Catholic Church*, put us to the test and, in retrospect, I fear we failed. Appearing on the "Phil Donahue Show," Ginder identified himself as a homosexual, suggesting that one in three priests was homosexual, and challenged the Church's teaching on various areas of human sexuality.

The response of the Church was to remove Fr. Ginder's faculties. The director of the Delaware Valley Office for Television and Radio called Ginder's remarks "scandalous and irresponsible." In response to Ginder's allegation about the number of homosexual clergy, the same diocesan official, Fr. Leo McKenzie, said, "Unsubstantiated and unjustified charges do irreparable harm to the work and reputations of thousands of virtuous and dedicated priests." (Fr. McKenzie, you will recall, was just arrested in the gay district of New Orleans for propositioning a male vice squad officer in a porno bookstore.)

Fighting for his faculties, Fr. Ginder wrote a remarkably audacious letter to Bishop Vincent Leonard, Ordinary of the diocese, in which he pleaded: "But why the uproar? Is it because the *vulgus* somehow consider the very condition of homosexuality a personal disgrace, and stubbornly refuse to accept the notion of a continent homosexual? They will contemplate the concept of homosexuality so long as it remains remote from them as in historical personages. . . .

"When the viewer is abruptly confronted with the Roman Catholic priest, the very pillar of propriety and examplar of respectability in his own community, happily proclaiming himself homosexual, albeit continent, that viewer is immediately subject to an emotional conflict that is all but unendurable.

"And this I intended. It is time for the public to grow up and face the truth that the estimated 15–20 million homosexuals in America constitute a cross-cut through every level of society from top to bottom. I meant to shake them up and set them thinking. Just off-hand, I could name at least 10 of our Pittsburgh priests who are homosexual and I dare say you could name three times as many. Of the Hierarchy . . ." At this point, Ginder broke the polite silence by naming bishops, living and dead, who he said "were well known for years in the gay underground as homosexuals, practicing or otherwise, with clear proof from lawyers and physicians still living."

It has been nearly four years since Ginder sent that letter to Bishop Leonard and thirty-two others, including Phil Donahue, Andrew Greeley, six American cardinals, the Apostolic Delegate and the officers of Dignity. We all, for one reason or another, greeted the letter similarly—with raised eyebrows and deep sighs. Perhaps worst of all, we greeted it with silence.

Ginder was being reckless, we thought. He won't get away with it. We've worked too hard to build a reputation of respect. Better put some distance between him and us. He's a political liability.

Richard Ginder might well have been a political liability at the time. He had been arrested six years prior on several charges of sodomy with adolescents. Yet, he was correct when he said the American public needed to be shaken up to get them thinking. He confronted the Church with its hypocrisy and for so doing was publicly attacked by a closeted Church official. He sent out a call for help and was politely denied assistance by those of us who claimed to be the official channel of communication between homosexuals and their Church.

Perhaps if we had fought the suspension of Ginder's faculties by clamoring in his behalf, we might have lost our reputation for politeness but gained some ground in the battle against complicity. Maybe if we had put our good name and reputation on the line with Richard, we could have built a powerful political force among gay Christians which would make Church leaders think twice before they dare to remove people like Fr. Paul Shanley from his ministry to sexual minorities; forbid retreats for gay women religious and remove qualified lesbians from executive posts merely for being gay.

It might even be true that if we had had the fortitude back then to support the effort to confront the Church with the high number of homosexuals among its spiritual leaders, the bishop would possibly have had fewer mourners and testimonies but the Episcopal priest and the Catholic Brother would be alive today, loving themselves as God intended.

Obviously, I'm still wrestling with it. I hope others are too.

◆
FORGIVENESS

February 1981

An Evangelical Christian theologian once told me that active homosexuals "who turn to the Bible for salvation are looking down the barrel of a shotgun." The laws of God are clear, he insisted, and unflinching.

The man in question was one of many hundreds of thousands who rallied around Anita Bryant in 1977 and joined *Newsweek* magazine in declaring her "God's Crusader." As her husband Bob phrased it, Anita had "put on the armor of God." In her own words, she was a modern day Deborah.

Today, the former national symbol of the perfect Christian wife and mother is divorced, recovering from a dangerous duet with drugs and alcohol and angry about the "fundamentalists who have become so legalistic and letter-bound to the Bible." Undoubtedly, she, too, is considered by her former friends to be foolishly encouraging God's double-barreled wrath.

Yet, as reported in the December, 1980, issue of *Ladies Home Journal*, Anita Bryant believes "in the long run, God will vindicate me." And so do I.

Like Rep. Robert Bauman (R-MD), who championed the fight against civil rights for homosexuals during the day and allegedly solicited sex in gay bars at night, Anita Bryant got caught between her own reality and the way she was taught things ought to be. She says that from the very beginning her marriage was a disaster, but she nonetheless wrote books, like *Mine Eyes Have Seen the Glory*, in which she told one million readers how happy she and Bob were in their nuclear Christian family. She wanted to have a happy marriage "so badly that I only shared the good parts."

By day she posed with her husband and children for pictures in front of their living room altar and decried gay civil rights as a threat to the American family. At night she fought bitterly with Bob, ridiculed him in front of friends, flirted with strangers and massaged her guilt with Valium. "When some people feel a total inadequacy in themselves, they feel threatened and jealous," she told the *Journal*.

Anita Bryant's major turnabout on such questions as gay civil rights and feminist issues hasn't received the attention it deserves from the nation's media. Perhaps that is because the airwaves are now jammed with the loud warnings of Anita's former supporters—the politicized Born Again fundamentalists—that Ronald Reagan and the new Congress had better listen to the Word of God and the Moral Majority and stay on the far right on such issues as busing, welfare, the ERA, civil rights and SALT II.

It's a shame because I believe Anita Bryant has been called upon to deliver a message of major significance. It seems to me that her conversion from celebrated intolerance to a philosophy of live and let live is a clear indictment of the self-righteous and a promise of forgiveness. It is a warning not to take yourself too seriously or God's embracing love too lightly. It is an invitation to accept yourself as flawed though intrinsically good and to look not into the barrel of a shotgun but into the welcoming arms of affirmation.

"I never dreamed what I feared most could happen to me," confided Anita. "But divorce is a part of life, you know, and we all are imperfect." In her pain, Anita came to discover that homosexuality is a part of life too, as are the concerns of women. "As for gays, the church needs to be more loving, unconditionally, and willing to see these people as human beings, to minister to them and try to understand them," she said.

While it isn't always true, I frequently find that I am more comfortable with people who are outside of approbation than with those whose lives seem to mirror society and fundamental churches' ideals. Those who are able to lay claim to their own pain, their uniqueness, their deviation from the norm seem to share generally the same experience of a loving God that I experience. They seem more able to go beyond the law and tradition and be in touch with the human experience. People who suffer aren't as prone to put other people in boxes, such as divorced Catholic, homosexual, welfare recipient, women's libber. They tend more to ask questions than to shoot from the hip. They talk honestly about their own feelings and abhor hypocrisy.

Jesus abhorred hypocrisy. In fact, He spoke out against it more frequently and with more vehemence than on any other human conduct. Hypocrites, for Him, were those persons who pretended to be something other than they were. Hypocrites were the law-givers and the law-quoters who denied their own experiences as flawed people.

Anita Bryant and Robert Bauman are two recent examples of individuals who publicly denied their private pain and puffed-up images of propriety to cover their flaws and receive social sanction. They became heroes to law-quoters and others who didn't trust God's embrace. Their charades caused more havoc in their own lives and in the lives of countless others who were scourged by their actions and their words, all in the name of God. "This is not my battle, it's God's battle," Anita told Dade County voters.

I knew the campaign against my civil rights was not God's battle, at least not my God's. Nor was it God's battle when people waved their Bibles in defiance of Charles Darwin or burned crosses on the lawns of Jews or beat up antiwar demonstrators or voted against the ordination of women. The God that I know isn't being talked about on Jerry Falwell's television show or in fundraising letters from Born Again groups which quote Corinthians to raise money against human rights. That used to be Anita Bryant's God but it doesn't seem to be anymore.

"God says the wages of sin are death," she told *Playboy* magazine in 1978, "and one little sin brings on another. . . . It just gets worse as it goes on. You go further and further down the drain and it just becomes so perverted and you get into alcohol and drugs and it's so rotten that many . . . end up committing suicide."

Back then she was talking about homosexuality. Two years later, she confided that her marriage was so bad she was taking heavy doses of pills and alcohol and one night would have committed suicide had she not thrown her pills down the drain the evening before. Two years later, she talks about a God I experienced after attempting suicide because my life didn't conform to the letter of the law.

"Fundamentalists have their heads in the sand," Anita now states. "The church is sick right now and I have to say I'm even part of that sickness. . . . They thought they could get me under their thumb, that I had such a responsibility to my 'righteous-leader' image, they thought that I would stay in that marriage. Well, I just couldn't hack it."

Welcome to the human race, Anita. Welcome to the world of the socially stigmatized, religiously ostracized human outcasts with whom Jesus, to the astonishment of law-quoters, preferred to walk.

For me, being an adult Christian is letting go of your fear of what the Church, the news media or the neighbors have to say about your life. It's a commitment to love yourself because of those things which make you different and to enable others to love their uniqueness. Being an adult Christian is a commitment to God that you will do your best to grow to your full potential, to embrace your humanity, to live life fully, to be a channel of encouragement and forgiveness in the world, to be honest, caring, involved and hopeful. It isn't easy being an adult Christian. It can be quite painful to be true to yourself.

"Of course, I know I'm going to hurt some more until the healing has time to work," says Anita. "But anyway, God loves me now right where I am." And so do I.

LISTENING
TO THE VOICE
WITHIN

March 1985

These can be dark and dreary times for many gay men and lesbians. For some people in our developing community, the events of these days even prompt moments of despair; of angry denunciations of being gay; of periodic longings for the security of the life they remember having before coming out of the closet.

The reasons for these feelings of anxiety are numerous and certainly understandable. Some of us, for instance, live in cities in which 60 percent of the beds in our hospitals' intensive-care units are occupied by persons with AIDS. We've lost good friends. We live in fear of losing others and of contracting AIDS ourselves. We're confused and alarmed.

Some of us live in states where moronic legislators speak carelessly of quarantining us in the public interest. Our local authorities seek to close our bathhouses and, although we may not be patrons of the baths, we wonder where they will stop. We're frightened and angry.

Some of us make our home in places where our neighbors

and our associates voted overwhelmingly to rescind our rights to employment. Some of us go to school in a place where straight students have sold hundreds of "Fagbusters" sweatshirts. Some of us live in towns where antigay violence is dramatically on the rise. We're shocked and we're depressed.

"Why did we ever leave the closet?" some of us ask. "What did we accomplish by coming out? At least we were safe when we pretended we were straight," some of us argue. "Even if it wasn't a perfect life, it was better to be safe passing for straight than to die out of the closet."

If we gay people listen carefully, we can hear other voices of history echo our anxiety.

When the Jews left Egypt, many of them did so with mixed emotions. They were excited by the sense of independence and self-determination which Moses promised them, but they were also frightened of the unknown. When they realized that Pharaoh and his army were rapidly pursuing them, some of them yelled at Moses, "Why did you do this to us? Why did you bring us out of Egypt? Did we not tell you this in Egypt when we said, 'Leave us alone. Leave us serve the Egyptians'? Far better for us to be the slaves of the Egyptians than to die in the desert."

Moses was probably hurt and confused by the frightened and angry responses of his people. Had he made a mistake in leaving Egypt? Was it better to be a slave? Why had he left in the first place?

It was the voice which had led Moses out of Egypt and it was the voice in which he ultimately placed his trust. The voice which led Moses and the Jews out of slavery is the same voice which led all gay men and women out of the closet. It is the same voice which whispered a dream to Martin Luther King, Jr. The voice which led an entire nation of Jews into a forty-year wandering in the desert is the same voice which led Gandhi to burn his English-made clothes; which led Caesar Chavez to politically organize his family and friends in the vineyards of California; which led Margaret Sanger to defy the law by providing birth control information to women.

The voice which speaks is the voice of God, which is the voice of life, which is the voice of self-affirmation. Moses heard the voice say "I am what I am." Albin clears the stage in *La Cage*

Aux Folles to proclaim "I am what I am." The voice within is a constant but generally subtle longing to live life fully and equally; to live life authentically and to die knowing that you have bloomed to your full potential.

The voice within is a person's best friend. It is also a troublemaker. The voice within sings an anthem of independence. Listening to it can make you feel dissatisfied with the way things are. Listening to it can prompt you to do and say things you never imagined were within you. Following its call to action can create all sorts of trouble. Family and friends will say, "You've *changed*." Employers will get nervous that you are getting out of line. Priests and rabbis will begin warning you of the sins of pride and reminding you of the perils of heresy.

People who listen to the voice almost always lose the security with which society had rewarded them for staying in line; for staying in Egypt; for staying on the plantation; for staying in the closet. When you listen to the voice within and decide to leave Egypt in the hope of finding a homeland, pharaohs chase you with their armies, voters take away your rights, college jocks mock you and people call you names, such as "militant," "radical," "avowed" and "troublemaker."

There is no story in the history of humankind in which people have listened to the voice within without suffering. All growth requires pain. Any time people have demanded that the world make room for their being, society has responded with the likes of Jerry Falwell, Jessie Helms, Cal Thomas and the other pharaohs with whom we currently deal.

Likewise, every time there is a troublemaking move out of captivity into liberation, there have always been and will always be nagging doubts, fears and anxieties among the liberated and among those called to liberation. Surely there were Jews who stayed in Egypt, just as there are women who curse feminism and as there are closeted homosexuals who hate the movement because it threatens their security. For every gay man or lesbian who has left the closet but at times wishes he or she hadn't, there are black people in history who periodically wished they hadn't left the security of the plantation and Indians who wished that the English had not granted their country its independence. Self-determination is an awesome challenge and it is natural to feel doubts and fears.

Though these can be dark and dreary times for many gay men and lesbians, these times will pass. Our generation has been tapped to lead the modern liberation movement while at the same time cope with the horrors of AIDS. Previous generations have been tapped to cope with the horrors of the Crusades, the Inquisition, the witch trials, the Holocaust and the McCarthy era. All of them died in the desert rather than serve the Egyptians. All of us will probably die before the others reach the promised land, but the movement forward will continue, even if, at times, it is an undirected wandering.

Though these are dark and dreary times for many gay men and lesbians who periodically think about the comforts of the closet, the pharaoh and his armies are still not enough to keep people in captivity. "I came out at the beginning of this year," wrote a fifty-five-year-old stranger in a letter to me yesterday, "by telling my wife of 23 years and my two sons (21 and 22) that I am gay. I moved into an apartment. I have a very special friend with whom I hope a lasting relationship will develop. After so many years of living straight and being gay, I have now found a peace which I neither knew was possible nor had any hope of achieving."

Welcome to the desert, my friend.

SERENITY
VERSUS
SECURITY

June 1985

Hanging on the wall of our cabin is a hand-painted plate which my partner Ray and I found in the basement of an antique shop and which captures for us the essence of our struggle as gay men today.

The molded three-dimensional scene is that of an elderly woman asleep in a comfortable chair in front of the fireplace. At her feet are a dozing dog and cat. On the table in front of her is a pot of tea. The drapes behind her are open, allowing the sun to pour into the room.

"She looks so secure," I said as we sat with the lights out one evening, the room lit by a fire and a candle beside the plate. "No," I said, correcting myself, "she's not secure. She's *serene*." Ray lay back and nodded his approval. "Do you know what the difference is?" I asked excitedly, thrilled by my own observation. "Being *secure* means feeling safe from all of those horrible heterosexuals and self-hating homosexuals out there who cause us pain. But being *serene* means that you aren't even thinking about them. You don't need to be safe from something you don't allow to affect you."

For the last several years, Ray and I have invested a lot of time, energy and money attempting to become secure. Undoubtedly, we will continue to do so, insofar as we both feel unsafe, and it is easier to buy security than it is to work for serenity. But it is serenity which will enable us to quit hurting, to quit being angry and to quit feeling unsafe.

I'm still hurting. I'm a self-affirmed eleven-year veteran of the gay and lesbian movement, a certified sex counselor, a sex educator and a generally happy man, but deep inside of me, at the soul of my being, there is a horrible gnawing pain. It's a pain which often prompts me to drink too much. It's a pain which can prompt me to cry silent tears when no one else is around and to occasionally lie awake at night as others sleep soundly. It's a hurt which sometimes makes me very angry.

I say I'm *still* hurting because like every gay man or lesbian I know, I have been hurting since I was a child. I have been in pain and I have felt unsafe. I have always felt disenfranchised and vulnerable. My hurt resulted from wanting to be part of the group and knowing that no matter how good I was, how smart, how kind, how generous, I would never really fit in.

I thought that when I came out that the hurt would go away, but it didn't. I thought that the changes which resulted in this country from the black, Hispanic and women's movements, the Second Vatican Council, the Vietnam War and Watergate would eliminate the hurt, but they didn't. I thought that winning awards from heterosexuals and from the gay community, publishing a book, getting standing ovations from straight college students and working in the mayor's office would stop the pain, but they didn't. I thought growing older, becoming financially secure, contributing to Democratic candidates would make me feel safe, but they didn't.

I am a good man, a loyal and loving son and citizen. I smile a lot, say please and thank you and give money to people in need. My home is wonderfully embracing. My relationship with my lover is nourishing and inspiring. My bills are paid; my dog is well-trained; my lawn is mowed; my flowers are the envy of the neighborhood and I always put down the toilet seat when I'm finished, so why do I sometimes hurt so badly? And why am I so angry?

Should a thirty-seven-year-old man flip the bird at the sight of Ronald Reagan, Pope John Paul II, Massachusetts Governor Michael Dukakis, Jerry Falwell, Boston Cardinal Bernard Law, Sandra Day O'Connor and Eddie Murphy? Perhaps I'm not alone. How many of you cheered when you heard that the Pope was booed in the Netherlands? How many of you loved all of the heat Reagan took on his visit to Bitburg?

Besides raising the middle index finger of my right hand with more frequency, I also swear more than I ever used to. Likewise, I am now more prone to climb on soapboxes, even with my friends. Just the other day, we were all having a fun time when someone raised the subject of gay foster parents. The allegedly liberal governor of Massachusetts, Michael Dukakis, recently ruled that gay men and lesbians ought not to be foster parents because the children deserve to be placed in a "normal" setting. Without prompting, I took the stage and reminded us all that children are always used by bigots to cloak their motives. Did not Anita Bryant call her hate-mongering "Save Our Children"? And what did family members murmur when our Greek Christian governor married his Jewish wife a few years ago and later adopted her son? How long ago was it that "decent" people opposed interfaith and interracial marriages "because of the children"?

I am deeply hurt when the governor publicly declares that my home is not as safe, that my love is not as nurturing, ultimately that my life is not as worthy as his or as that of any other person who happens to have been born heterosexual. I am hurt because I am once again reminded that no matter how unjust, an ignorant heterosexual majority won't let me be part of the group. I am also very angry because, as is so often true with antigay pronouncements from members of the Church's hierarchy, the governor's decision denied his own experiences and served to further hurt countless numbers of innocent people.

Perhaps the reason that I flip the bird, swear and climb on soapboxes more often than I used to is that I am tired of playing silly games with politicians and Church leaders who have to twist the truth to justify their prejudices. Perhaps I am angrier today than I was ten years ago because I know more about the hypocrisy which surrounds these antigay statements and positions. However, in addition to being angrier than I was a few years ago, I'm also smarter. I'm smart enough to know that the trouble with being angry with the governor, Reagan, John Paul II, Falwell and others like them is that anger takes a greater toll on me than it does on them. When I'm angry, I don't taste food, and they enjoy their meals. When I'm angry, I toss and turn at night, and they sleep well. Worst of all, my anger costs me money. I'm back in therapy to deal with my anger, to become whole, to become serene, and I don't think I should have to pay the price for the effects of their ignorance or, as the case may be, their bigotry.

I will undoubtedly go to my grave with my inner hurt. I can't undo the memories of alienation and fear I have from growing up in this country at this time. They are a part of me and I will probably shed a few more silent tears of frustration at the injustice of it all. But, if I am going to sit with Ray next to the woman in the chair, asleep in front of the fire; if I am going to become serene, I need to get rid of the anger. I need to forgive and not forget.

Forgiving means that I either attempt to understand that Reagan, John Paul, Falwell, Dukakis and the others are sad results of their backgrounds and the choices they have made in their lives, or I walk away from them. If I stay angry at them, they will follow me into my living room and prevent me from enjoying the dozing pets, sunshine and hot tea. For my own sake, I need to let go of them; to build my own space which they can't affect. But I won't forget!

I need to work at forgiving them but I will also work for their defeat in the next election or, at the very least, not contribute to or vote for them. I will work to forgive them but I will also not drink their Coors beer, buy their comedy albums, give to their relief funds, line their parade routes or mourn their deaths.

Being serene means being "free from storms and unpleasant change"; it means utter calm and "unruffled repose." You can be serene and still hurt, but you can't be serene and be angry.

I'm not serene yet, but I'm working on it.

CELEBRATION

CELEBRATION

Right after the defeat of the gay civil rights ordinance in Dade County a decade ago, I debated a representative of Anita Bryant Ministries on a television talk show. The conservative hostess of the program opened with "This is Gay Pride Week, although I don't know why anyone would be proud to be a homosexual." I smiled. She frowned. Every year since the Stonewall Rebellion in June 1969, considered the birth of the modern gay and lesbian rights movement, thousands of men and women have marched down the streets of some of our nation's largest cities for the annual gay pride celebration. There are often floats and sometimes marching bands, always balloons and bold banners and dependably heartfelt cheers. This is the one day of the year during which gay men and women head into the streets as a community to make joyful noise that they are proud to be gay. Some of the people each year are marching for the first time and it is an experience they cherish for the rest of their lives. For others, it is a traditional pilgrimage, a cultural ritual like St. Patrick's Day, which they wouldn't consider missing. For everyone, it is a day for smiling. At the end of 1987, hundreds of thousands of lesbians and gay men assembled in

Washington, D.C., for a monumental demonstration of solidarity, anguish over AIDS and celebration of gay pride. It was a remarkable event which made me smile particularly broadly. I smiled for me. I smiled for my friends who had died of AIDS. I smiled for that befuddled talk show host back in Dade County. I smile because I'm proud to be me and I smile a lot.

◆

PROUD
ABOUT WHAT?

June 1983

Now that we have rolled up our banners, swept up our confetti and tucked away our Lesbian and Gay Pride T-shirts for another year, a bit of reflecting on our celebration seems in order. What are the particulars which make us proud about the gay and lesbian presence in the world?

I'm proud of our resilience. Most of us grow up in families which are afraid to know our secret, go through schools which deny our existence, head into jobs which encourage our duplicity, encounter doctors and ministers and other honored healers who seek to transform us and we nonetheless survive!

I'm proud of our history of heroes and heroines who, one by one, throughout time, pounded, shoved, scratched and oiled the hinges of our closet door.

I'm proud of how we gay men and lesbians today hang together when we deal with tragedies such as AIDS. Though we're the orphaned children of the civil rights movement; though we may have no family, church or other institutional support, we time and time again baffle our enemies by our ability to dig in, generously donate our time and money to take care of our own and sacrifice our private lives to make sure that no one who travels with us walks unassisted.

I'm proud of those lesbians and gay people of color and disability who struggle to stick with the movement when all too often able-bodied gay white men pretend they don't exist, or, worse yet, pretend that our agenda meets their needs. And I'm proud of those able-bodied gay white men who struggle to rid themselves of a limited agenda and world view.

I'm proud of those lesbian mothers and gay fathers who choose to fight for custody when they feel they would be the best parent to raise their children.

I'm proud of those gay and lesbian children who hold on to the dream of one day building a healthy and secure environment for themselves.

I'm proud of those gay and lesbian college students who don't give up when their posters are repeatedly torn down and of those who hold strong when their university refuses to recognize them as a legitimate group. They spend what little money they have to pay for the telephone, supplies and office space other student groups get for free.

I'm proud of those office workers who refuse to play charades with their peers and who therefore endure the daily cold shoulder rather than the daily lies. They know that if someone has to be uncomfortable about their being gay, it ought not to be them.

I'm proud of those gay men and lesbians who have gay literature and art prominently displayed in their homes and who do not put them under the bed when family arrives for a visit. It takes a while to understand that one's home is one's only space for free expression. If visitors are made uncomfortable by our self-expression, visitors should not visit.

I'm proud of those gay men and lesbians who recently marched in their first Pride Parade, even if it was in straw hat and sunglasses; of those who have bought their first lesbian or gay periodical or book from a straight sales clerk; of those who have cautiously stepped foot into their first gay bar or attended their first meeting of a gay organization. I know how frightened they were and how much courage it took.

I'm proud of all those gay men and women who have written letters to the editor to protest inaccurate or nonexistent reporting on our community and of those who have made phone calls to station managers to compliment a sensitive portrayal of our issues. These gay people know the media must serve everyone.

I'm proud of the volunteers who staff our hotlines. They give up their free time so that lonely, frightened and often desperate people will have at least one friendly voice and open ear to rely upon. I know that the abuse they endure from those who call with death threats and obscene messages takes its toll.

I'm proud of those lesbians and gay men who head up our local and national organizations. They are paid little, if anything, and put in far more time than is good for their health. Rarely are they adequately thanked. Too often are they senselessly criticized. Nevertheless, they have a dream and they are willing to sacrifice for it.

I'm proud of those gay Christians and Jews who won't give up on their institutions. Their's is a courage and faith even the churches will one day honor. And I'm proud of those who have held on to their spiritual beliefs though not their institutional ties. They have had the nerve to walk it alone.

I'm proud of those who are still willing to take to the streets to draw attention to injustice against gay people and of those who are willing to work the system for change. I am most proud when both approaches are affirmed by gay men and lesbians as being choices and not mandates for everyone.

I'm proud of our free press which began as mimeographed sheets with misspelled words and has matured into a sophisticated network of independent professional periodicals which inform us, challenge us and enable us to express our feelings.

And I'm proud of our lesbian and gay authors and poets and photographers and painters and recording artists and of our gay and lesbian publishing houses and record companies and radio shows, all of whom give us the sights and sounds of gay and lesbian celebration every day of the year.

These are only some of the particulars which make me proud about the gay and lesbian presence in the world. There are many more. I encourage you to think about them during a quiet moment. I encourage nongay people to think about them too. Perhaps if they were to become aware of the treasures we hold and offer generously, they would add their own confetti to next year's pageant.

◆

ABOUT
THE AUTHOR

BRIAN MCNAUGHT is an award-winning freelance writer, educational consultant and lecturer. From June 1982 to February 1984, he served as the mayor of Boston's liaison to the gay and lesbian community. In that capacity, he worked to ensure full and equal access to city services for Boston's gay citizens, conducted a citywide study of constituent needs, coordinated the city's response to the AIDS epidemic and trained police, fire and other service providers. Mr. McNaught is featured in the popular educational video, *A Conversation with Brian McNaught On Being Gay*, and has spoken at dozens of colleges and universities and at numerous professional and community gatherings throughout North America. He is certified with the American Association of Sex Educators, Counselors and Therapists.

Upon receiving his journalism degree from Marquette University in 1970, Mr. McNaught was hired as a conscientious objector by *The Michigan Catholic*, the newspaper of the Archdiocese of Detroit. While there, he worked as a reporter, wrote an award-winning weekly column, became a popular host of a diocesan television program and was a frequent speaker at Catholic youth functions.

In 1974, Mr. McNaught came out in the *Detroit News* as an affirmed homosexual. His column was immediately dropped by the Catholic newspaper. After a water fast in reparation of the

Church's sins against gay men and women, which ended when the local bishops pledged to work to educate the clergy about homosexuality, he was fired from his other responsibilities at the paper.

The founder of the Detroit chapter of Dignity, an organization of gay and concerned Catholics, Mr. McNaught represented and successfully lobbied for gay Catholics at the U.S. Bishops' 1976 bicentennial conference, "A Call to Action."

In 1976, Mr. McNaught received the Catholic Press Association's Journalism Award for Best Magazine Article of the Year. The article, "The Sad Dilemma of the Gay Catholic," appeared in the *U.S. Catholic* (August 1975). Other religious publications to which he has contributed include the *National Catholic Reporter* and the *Witness*, a monthly magazine of the Episcopal Church, for which he has served as guest editor. In 1979, he was as a consultant to and is featured in the Guidance Associates' filmstrip presentation, *The Hidden Minority: Homosexuality in Our Society*. He has also been a consultant to the National Council of Churches in young adult ministry.

Mr. McNaught's syndicated column, "A Disturbed Peace" appeared in the gay press from 1974 to 1986. He has also contributed chapters to numerous college texts and gay and lesbian anthologies, including *Humanistic Psychology: A Source Book* (Prometheus Books, 1978), *Positively Gay* (Celestial Arts, 1978) and *Gay Life* (Doubleday, 1986). He has written for a variety of periodicals, including the *Advocate*, the *Humanist*, *In Touch*, *SIECUS Report* and *The Boston Globe*.

In 1979, Mr. McNaught received the Margaret Sanger Award from the Institute for Family Research and Education at Syracuse University for his contribution to the general public's understanding of homosexuality. In 1978 and 1979, he was named one of the Outstanding Young Men of America. He has twice been cited for honors by the gay and lesbian community.

Mr. McNaught serves as a consultant to the Cape Ann (MA) AIDS Task Force, is a volunteer buddy with the AIDS Action Committee of Boston and is on the Board of Directors of HAWK, (Help for Abused Women and Their Children). He works out of his home in Gloucester, Massachusetts, which he shares with Ray Struble, his partner in life since 1976.